"Vera Brennan applies the timeless wisdom of Solomon to today's young adults, to equip them to make the best choices for their present and future. She challenges singles to discover real truth and discern God's will for making the most of their time, developing solid friendships, and living a life of faith. She brings her experience as a mother, pre-marriage counselor, and young adult facilitator to engage young people to think deeply and study the word with open minds."

— ***Karen Whiting*** (*www.karenwhiting.com*)
Writing coach, author of thirty books,
international speaker, and former television host

"Every young adult can benefit from reading through Proverbs and this devotional is especially good for the current young adult population."

— ***Laurie Atz***
Young adult pastor at First Assembly of God
Chi Alpha Director, Purdue Fort Wayne
and Indiana Tech

"Proverbs is a timeless book that is as relevant today as it was when it was written over 2700 years ago. However, when you combine an ancient document like Proverbs, with the pen and the heart of a modern woman like Vera, you have a manuscript that powerfully touches the heart of all those who dare to read it."

— *Scott Volk*
Founder and director, Together for Israel

"Vera Brennan's literary offering *God's GPS* taken from the book of Proverbs is written simply, but surely a life changer! Each of her seventy devotionals is encouraging and a reflection of her devoted life to God. Although it is geared for young adults – I'm an 'oldie' and it spoke to me! I believe *God's GPS* will surely touch every reader's heart!"

— *June Volk*
Author of The God Who Answers by Fire,
Drinking from the Wells of Salvation with Study
Guide, and The Secret Place and teacher
and television cohost, Scottsdale, AZ

"This devotional, meant for single young adults like myself, encourages me to dive into the Word, specifically the book of Proverbs, and seek for myself what it says. It challenges me to meditate on how its wisdom applies and affects my life and my relationship with God. And as an added plus: I always felt pressured to read Proverbs but when reading it in The Passion Translation, the Bible version used in *God's GPS*, wisdom took on a whole new significance."

— *Ciera Miller*
Missionary kid raised in the Philippines, English major
at Regents University, and student chaplain for
the cross country/track and field eam

GOD'S GPS

GOD'S GPS

A JOURNEY THROUGH PROVERBS

VERA G. BRENNAN

ILLUMIFY
MEDIA.COM

GOD'S GPS

Published by
Illumify Media Global
www.IllumifyMedia.com
"Let's bring your book to life!"

Paperback ISBN: 978-1-959099-11-6

Typeset by Art Innovations (http://artinnovations.in/)
Cover design by Debbie Lewis

Printed in the United States of America

CONTENTS

Foreword   xiii

Acknowledgments   xv

Devo 1   The Prologue   1

Devo 2   The Wisdom of a Father   3

Devo 3   Wisdom's Warning   5

Devo 4   Searching for Wisdom   7

Devo 5   Wisdom, the Way of the Pure   9

Devo 6   The Rewards of Wisdom   11

Devo 7   Wisdom's Guidance   13

Devo 8   Wisdom's Correction   15

Devo 9   Wisdom's Blueprints   17

Devo 10   Wisdom, Our Hiding Place   19

Devo 11   Wisdom in Relationships   21

Devo 12   A Father's Instruction   23

Devo 13   Two Pathways   25

Devo 14   Healing Words   27

Devo 15   Watch Where You're Going   29

Devo 16   Avoid Promiscuity   31

Devo 17   Sex Reserved for Marriage   33

Devo 18   Words of Wisdom   35

Devo 19   Life Lessons   37

Devo 20   Seven Things God Hates   39

Devo 21   Truth or Consequences   41

Devo 22   Wisdom, Your True Love   43

Devo 23   Wisdom Calling   45

Devo 24   The Power of Wisdom   47

Devo 25   Wisdom in the Beginning   49

Devo 26   Wisdom Worth Waiting For   51

Devo 27   Wisdom's Feast   53

Devo 28   A Spirit Named Foolish   55

Devo 29   A Father Rejoices   57

Devo 30   A Mother Grieves   59

Devo 31   Living in Righteousness   61

Devo 32   It's Right to Live for God   63

Devo 33   Wisdom Means Being Teachable   65

Devo 34   Learning to Speak Wisely   67

Devo 35   Living Wisely   69

Devo 36   The House of Wisdom   71

Devo 37   Wisdom Far Better Than Wickedness   73

Devo 38   The Eyes of the Lord   75

Devo 39   Living an Ascended Life   77

Devo 40   Wisdom Exalts God   79

Devo 41   Living Like a King   81

Devo 42   Walking with Wisdom   83

Devo 43   Wisdom's Virtues   85

Devo 44   Wisdom Gives Life   87

Devo 45   Wisdom Exalted   89

Devo 46   Giving God's Way   91

Devo 47   Are You Living Wisely?   93

Devo 48   God Is the Source of Wisdom   95

Devo 49   How to Live a Life of Wisdom   97

Devo 50   Sayings of the Wise Sages   99
Devo 51   Wisdom Will Protect You   101
Devo 52   Wisdom's Warning   103
Devo 53   Revelation from the Wise   106
Devo 54   Wisdom Practices Self-Control   108
Devo 55   Don't Be a Fool   110
Devo 56   Don't Be Lazy   112
Devo 57   Watch Your Words   114
Devo 58   Heed Wisdom's Warnings   116
Devo 59   Lovers of God   118
Devo 60   Don't Be Stubborn   120
Devo 61   You Can't Argue with a Fool   122
Devo 62   The Mysterious Sayings of Agur   124
Devo 63   Six Questions   126
Devo 64   A Pure Heart Is Filled with God's Word   128
Devo 65   Four Mysteries   130
Devo 66   Four Intolerable Things   132
Devo 67   Four Creatures Small and Wise   134
Devo 68   Four Stately Things   136
Devo 69   Inspired Words   138
Devo 70   The Radiant Bride   140
Devo 71   The Journey Is Over   142

About the Author   213
Endnotes   215

FOREWORD

Any book that you ever hold in your hands has the potential to change your life. Few things compare to the power of the written word, and I believe that this book is no different, as it is written by a woman who is loved and respected by many.

I met Vera Brennan nearly fifty years ago as a young boy living in a Christian community in Northern Minnesota. Vera was a few years older than I and always stood out as a woman of wisdom. So, when I picked up this book for the first time, one of the first things that caught my attention was that each devotional started with a quote from the book of Proverbs.

Proverbs is a timeless book that is as relevant today as it was when it was written over 2,700 years ago. However, when you combine an ancient document like Proverbs with the pen and the heart of a modern woman like Vera, you have a manuscript that powerfully touches the heart of all those who dare to read it.

As I went through each devotional, I was struck with both the simplicity as well as the profundity of each of the readings. Anyone can read and understand what is written on each page, but not everyone will take the challenge of applying it to their own life.

I want to personally encourage you to do one thing after reading each devotional, and that is this: take the "challenge" section seriously. Without doing that, you'll only be obtaining beneficial information. When you take the challenge section seriously, you'll also be setting yourself up for success and blessing in your life.

Our common enemy, the devil, will do everything he can to try to hijack your walk with our Lord. This book has the potential for being a tool in your hands to gain the victory over the one who is out to destroy those who desire to serve their King. It is my prayer that you'll be as encouraged and strengthened as I was when I read each devotional and took each challenge seriously.

Scott Volk
Founder and director, Together for Israel

WHO CAME ALONG FOR THE JOURNEY

This was not a lone-ranger production.

In the summer of 2019, I attended the Greater Philadelphia Christian Writers Conference. There I participated in a workshop with Peter Lundell, who taught me, among other things, about alpha and beta readers. Alpha readers are folks whose writing ability you respect, and beta readers are those in your target audience. It sounded like wisdom to me. So . . .

Meet the team.

Alpha readers:

Paul Brennan, my beloved and my biggest support, also happens to be a good writer.

Naomi Maddox Harris, my niece, contributed her writing skill as well as her eye for a different perspective.

Beta readers:

Hope Skoda, whose mom was my best friend in my Brooklyn, New York, days, always pointed out when I was too harsh or lacked clarity.

Trevor McKorkle, who came on board during the pandemic via the recommendation of a mutual friend, gave the male perspective. He, too, challenged my writing style as well as my approach. But his wedding in July 2021 disqualified him as a single young adult.

Nate Warwick, who replaced Trevor, was the result of a sovereign nudge from God. Nate, who was a recent graduate with a degree in childhood education, critiqued with the eye of a scholar.

Thanks to June Volk who introduced me to The Passion Translation of the Bible.

Special thanks also to Karen Whiting who helped me in ways too numerous to count.

Of course, thanks to the staff at Illumify Media, who made God's GPS a reality.

And last but never least, I owe this publication to the author of God-sized tasks, Jesus Himself!

WHY I WROTE THIS DEVOTIONAL

Some thirty years ago, I married a man named Paul who had a ten-year-old son. I watched this child, who was basically born and raised Christian, begin to slip away from his faith as a senior in high school. From that point forward the slip became a swift slide, but he continued to see himself as a Christian and believed there was absolutely nothing abnormal about his behavior. His dad and I knew otherwise; we fervently prayed. Finally, by God's mercy, he escaped the downward spiral he'd been on. By this time, he had become a tattoo artist and a talented one at that.

Tattoo artists in the continental United States are not required to be licensed, so our son made it a practice to travel from state to state and work as a guest artist for a week or so at established tattoo parlors. It was an easy gig, as his gift opened the doors, but it meant bunking wherever he could find a place to stay, and church attendance was not a priority for him. Observing his lifestyle, Paul and I then began to pray for him to "settle" where he could become part of a local church and have Christian accountability. Shortly thereafter, he called us from California to share that he felt his wandering days were over! We were thrilled! I asked how long he would be there. The whole month of December, he replied, while he waited to go to Hawaii, a state which required tattoo artists to be licensed, and the test was offered only once a year in January.

Well, we suggested, "settle" there for the month and attend a local church—see it as "home" for the next thirty days. He took our advice. It so happened that the pastor of the church he chose to attend encouraged the congregation to read a chapter a day from Proverbs. Our son went for the challenge. It had a profound effect on his life.

When I decided to write this devotional, I asked him what he had gleaned from that **challenge:**

- Even though he never doubted the reality of God or that Jesus had died for his sins, Christianity had no meaning beyond that. He was a believer but not a follower.
- Proverbs confirmed for him that what we get from the Father is superior to what we get from man.
- Proverbs hits on real-life topics.
- True wisdom shows us how to apply knowledge—in other words, how to navigate life.
- God is the true source of wisdom.
- God's download is for the moment as well as for the future.

It convinced me: other single young adults needed to hear this as well, and the idea of writing God's GPS would be worth my time!

Before You Begin

So, you bought this devotional—or someone gave it to you. Well, you are in for a life-changing read, if you're up to the challenge, because this devotional is dedicated to you—the single young adult. It follows the book of Proverbs, which was written, for the most part, by Solomon, son of King David of ancient Israel. Considered the wisest and wealthiest man who ever lived, Solomon had you in mind when he wrote Proverbs. He desired to share his wisdom, "to give youth [that's you] the understanding of their design and destiny" (Proverbs 1:4). However, the wisdom of Solomon is meant for all ages in any circumstance, so if you are not single or you're over the age of thirty-two, you are wise to join the ride.

Are you ready to dive in?

If so, then you need to know this devotional is not based on just any translation of the Bible. It is to be used in conjunction with reading from The Passion Translation (TPT).1 However, other translations and paraphrases can of course offer other angles to the picture. By all means, check them out.

So, you're picking up the gauntlet.

The first step: Get access to The Passion Translation: New Testament with Psalms, Proverbs and Song of Songs, Second Edition. Before you read each of the devotions in this book, read the entire section of Scripture that goes with it. For this is "the living Word of God, which is full of energy, and it pierces more sharply than a two-edged sword. . . . It interprets and reveals the true thoughts and secret motives of our hearts" (Hebrews 4:12). The life within each devotion is found in the Word.

Second: Prepare to be changed. With each devotion, there is a challenge meant for you to put into action the wisdom you are given. This is how you receive optimal benefit from this devotional. Think of it as how you get a pay raise from your boss or a good grade from your professor. Better yet, as James puts it, "Those who . . . respond to the truth they hear and are strengthened by it—they experience God's blessing in all that they do!" (James 1:25).

Finally: Plan to record your thoughts. There are seventy pages in the back of the devotional where you can do this. Just use two bookmarks—one for the reading and one for the recording. But a blank journal or simple notebook will also do. You will not want to forget what you hear directly from the Holy Spirit as you read and take action on the day's devotion. The Holy Spirit is the ultimate teacher, the one who knows you best and what you need to learn.

And I will join the Holy Spirit in praying for you. For I know it will take diligence and perseverance, but following through with the challenge for each devotion will be a decision you'll never regret.

PS. You may be wondering, Why are there seventy devotions? Don't most devotionals run thirty or sixty or 365 days? In an article entitled "Israel and the Meaning of 70," Dr. Elana Yael Heideman, executive director of the Israel Forever Foundation, explains that "70 is opportunity. 70 is potential. 70 represents completion, wholeness, the real thing."2 That being the case, why not go for it!

THE PROLOGUE

These proverbs will give you great skill to teach the immature and make them wise, to give youth the understanding of their design and destiny.
—PROVERBS 1:4

READ: PROVERBS 1:1–7

You are at the beginning of a whole new phase of living. The world is before you! You are faced with choosing what you'll do, where you'll go, and who you'll ask to join you. The possibilities are endless, obstacles few! You will be forming the foundation of your destiny. But before you make those choices, take time to read what Solomon has to say about "words of wisdom" (v. 1). Don't be stubborn, thinking you know it all. In these pages, you will be given the "keys" to unlock true knowledge, to be able to choose what is right, just, and fair. With the reading, choose to live in obedience to God, for then you will indeed gain the wisdom offered.

CHALLENGE: Make the decision, here at the onset, to read Proverbs with an open heart and mind. Make the decision to apply what you learn, asking the Lord to give you the specifics of how to do so. This means planning to read daily at a certain time in a specific place. Write your plan and then follow it. It will take discipline. However, as you discipline yourself to do this, it will become a delight, an appointment you will not want to miss.

THE WISDOM OF A FATHER

When peer pressure compels you to go with the crowd
. . . simply say, "No!"
—PROVERBS 1:10

READ: PROVERBS 1:8–19

I f you've ever been horseback riding, then you know that the "reins" are what you use to steer the horse in the desired direction. Whether you're still living at home or living on campus or sharing an apartment—whether you are beginning a degree or your first "real" job—your decisions (how you use the "reins" of life) will begin to matter more than in the past. Select carefully to whom you will listen. Choose wise counselors, those you respect. Think seriously about whom you are hanging out with—that includes contacts on social media—for you become, to a certain extent, like them. If you're fortunate enough to have a God-fearing (by "God" I mean the God of the Bible) loved one whom you respect, pay attention to their words. They are the "reins" you need. It will make the difference between success and destruction.

Destruction might start with something like this: when your roommate or classmate or office mate says, "Hey, there's a cool party at the lake," and adds with a wink, "Wine, women, and weed," or "Beer, boys and . . . brownies." Or when you're the new person on the job and an older employee suggests ways you can cheat the boss or hoodwink the customer, lining your pockets with the victim's assets. When these things happen, simply pull back on the "reins" and say, "No!" If you don't, you will gallop headlong into an ambush—into destruction.

CHALLENGE: What decisions are you currently facing? Are you being lured to follow the crowd? Whose advice, suggestions, opinions are you listening to? Do they line up with the wise counsel of God the Father? Use a Bible App and type in a key word related to your current choices to search what the Bible says. Record what you find. Talk to the Father about it before you make your decision.

WISDOM'S WARNING

Wisdom's song is not always heard in the halls of higher learning.
—PROVERBS 1:21

READ: PROVERBS 1:20–33

So, you have chosen to go to university, "the halls of higher learning" (v. 22). Well, beware. You are living in a post-Christian era. It is easy to fall prey to the philosophies of your professors. Even at a Christian institution, you can encounter theologians who no longer agree with the infallibility of Scripture. In fact, in the mid-1960s several proclaimed they were constructing a theology without God. The advances in science, they concluded, explained away the mysteries of nature. The cover story of the April 8, 1966, issue of TIME Magazine asked, "Is God Dead?" and their readers were outraged.[3] But now, in the twenty-first century, our culture considers God is not only dead but that He never was. He was a figment of our imagination. And the results? Look at our nation: Abortion legalized in some states up to the point of birth.[4] Same-gender marriages honored.[5] Mass shootings on the rise with people blaming the Second Amendment rather than the condition of the heart.[6] God says to those who have "turned a deaf ear" to [His] voice" and "laughed at [His] counsel," "You've made your own bed; now lie in it!" (vv. 24–25, 31). But those who listen to Him "will live undisturbed . . . confident and courageous . . . unafraid and sheltered" (v. 33). The choice is yours.

CHALLENGE: To what degree have you been exposed to the idea of the nonexistence of God or the rationalizing away of biblical principles such as the sins of homosexuality, abortion, murder, even lying? (Yes, liars are consigned to hell. See Revelation 21:8.) What is your stance on such trends? Do they agree with biblical standards? Is something enticing you to rewrite Scripture to support modern beliefs? Reread today's Proverbs passage and consider the results on a personal level of following these trends.

SEARCHING FOR WISDOM

Train your heart to listen when I speak.
—PROVERBS 2:2

READ: PROVERBS 2:1–15

Whether you are training to be a medic or a teacher or a nuclear scientist, a short order cook or a store clerk, it pays to listen to your instructor. It pays to remember what he or she tells you during your training. If there is anything you don't understand, ask. Research for yourself what you're being taught. Don't think you know it all. So, too, with every word the Lord gives. Not only accept His words, but treasure them, hide them in your heart, cry out for understanding. Hold on to every word He speaks in Scripture so that you may be empowered to make wise decisions. In so doing, you attain the wisdom you will need to walk into your destiny.

CHALLENGE: Reread this passage and note all the benefits that come from heeding the wisdom of the Lord. The greatest of these is the "fear of the Lord" (v. 5). To learn more about this concept, read Psalm 34:11–20. As you read, make note of any verses that speak to you. Your response will indicate that you do indeed fear the Lord; in fact, your respect for Him and your obedience to His Word is another way of saying you "fear the Lord."

GOING DEEPER: If you have time and interest, either now or at a later date, read the following verses to learn why the "fear of the Lord" is so important: Psalms 19:9; 25:14; 33:18; 34:7; 103:17; 111:10; 128:1. Select two that seem especially powerful to you. You could consider memorizing them or writing them out on a sticky note and placing them near your mirror. Note: the phrase "fear of the Lord" is not always found in the TPT, but the concept is the same.

WISDOM, THE WAY OF THE PURE

*Only wisdom can save you from the flattery of
the promiscuous woman—
she's such a smooth-talking seductress!*
—PROVERBS 2:16

READ: PROVERBS 2:16–22

This passage refers to the promiscuous "woman," but it also applies to the promiscuous "man." In fact, our current culture could be described as promiscuous. It declares that sexual intimacy is no more than a handshake, the way to top off an evening. There is no concern, other than STDs, to go from one relationship to the next or to have multiple relationships at the same time. It's okay to have children without marrying. In fact, you can even be intimate with someone from the same sex. But do not be deceived by these things, no matter who tells you otherwise, for

9

you will lose all you could have had. Do not even take one step in that direction—it is the "road to hell" (v. 18).

Instead, first develop a friendship with someone from the opposite sex. You may discover they are not the person for you. Even if you decide this is Mr. (or Miss) Right, only hold hands until he puts a ring on your finger. Then, once you're engaged, let your hugs mostly be from the side; otherwise, you're in danger of arousing the physical appetite. Besides, gentlemen, if you press her for sexual favors before you marry, and she tells you no, she'll keep telling you no in other areas once you put a wedding ring on her finger. She wants a man she can respect, one who loves her like Christ loves the church. It'll be easier for her to be holy devoted to him.

CHALLENGE: If you have taken the wrong path, get back on track now. Repent. And that means much more than sobbing, "I'm sorry." It's a 180-degree turn—from your way to His way. Repent first to yourself. Why to yourself first? If you don't think you've harmed yourself, your confession will be a farce. Afterward, repent to the Lord. There is forgiveness, for "if we freely admit our sins . . . , he will be faithful to forgive us every time" (1 John 1:9). As Romans 8:1 also tells us, "So now the case is closed. There remains no accusing voice of condemnation."

But if you have never taken the path of the promiscuous, or you did once and are now back on track, hold fast to that testimony. You show others there's another way, a better way, to "enjoy life to the fullest and . . . inherit their destinies" (v. 21).

THE REWARDS OF WISDOM

If you truly want a long and satisfying life, . . .
let your life be shaped by integrity,
with truth written upon your heart.
—PROVERBS 3:1, 3

READ: PROVERBS 3:1–4

"If you truly want a long and satisfying life" . . . (v. 1). There's no question about it: we all want to live a long and satisfying life. Do you want to "find favor . . . with both God and men" (v. 4)? Most of us do. But how do you receive these rewards? What is the secret to a lifetime of well-being? The answer is the same whether you were raised in a Christian home or have only recently become a follower of Jesus or may just be curious. That answer is to hold on to all you are being taught and have been taught in God's Word. His truth has always been and will always remain. "Every Scripture has been inspired by the Holy Spirit, the breath of God. It will empower you by its instruction and correction, giving you the strength to take the right direction and lead you deeper into the path of godliness. Then you will be God's servant, fully mature and perfectly prepared to fulfill any assignment God gives you" (2 Timothy 3:16–17). Be encouraged when you meditate on God's Word. He stamps eternity on the walls of your heart; with that, you cannot fail to live well.

CHALLENGE: If you are not already doing so, make a plan for a time and a place to meditate daily on the full counsel of God, not just Proverbs. Record what you learn; then ask the Lord how He would have you apply it. And, of course, carry out His instructions! Note: at the time of this writing, The Passion Translation does not exist for the whole Bible, so for some sections you will need to use another translation. In your reading, consider alternating between various sections, such as the Old Testament (history, poetry, prophecy) and the New Testament (the Gospels, Acts, the Epistles, and Revelation).

WISDOM'S GUIDANCE

*Trust in the Lord completely, and
do not rely on your own opinions."*
—PROVERBS 3:5

READ: PROVERBS 3:5–10

One of the pitfalls of adolescence is thinking we know it all. But usually, when we turn eighteen, we begin to realize there's still a whole lot more to learn to navigate life successfully. The right guide, one whom we can "trust . . . completely" (v. 5), is a necessity. That's the first thing we need to know. To whom or what do we turn when we need advice, when a decision needs to be made ASAP, when we are concerned or anxious or afraid? What we need then is to "become intimate" (v. 6) with the Lord, giving Him our undivided attention. Place your decisions and desires, your concerns and fears, in His hands, and then watch Him faithfully attend to every one. He will direct your path. Honor Him with your very best, and your life will "overflow with blessings" (v. 10).

13

CHALLENGE: Ask yourself, Do I trust in the Lord completely, or do I rely on my own opinions? Be honest with yourself. If you don't trust Him completely, ask yourself why. Take time to write out your reply. Note: I had been a follower of Christ for decades before I realized my go-to for decision making was my own opinion. I asked myself why and realized it was because God is portrayed as a father and my experience with my earthly father convinced me that fathers were not altogether trustworthy. I spent my childhood taking care of myself, then spent my young adult years carving out my own destiny. As an adult, I relied heavily on my own opinions and more than once came to regret the actions I'd taken. May you choose otherwise.

WISDOM'S CORRECTION

When the Lord God speaks to you,
never take his words lightly,
and never be upset when he corrects you.
—PROVERBS 3:11

READ: PROVERBS 3:11–18

It's very likely, when you were a child, your parents told you, "You're in time out for your own good." The Lord does the same, but His discipline is far better than what your parents gave. Unlike earthly parents, who sometimes correct out of anger or frustration, your heavenly Father only corrects from His "passionate love" for you (v. 12). His desire is to train you in the proper way to live, to develop His character in you. The fruit of His correction is wisdom, something which is more valuable than gold. It draws you into a "place of wholeness, . . . of untold blessings" (v. 17–18). Therefore "never be upset when [the Lord] corrects you" (v. 11).

CHALLENGE: Reread verses 13–18. Underline or write out the "untold blessings" you will have in finding true wisdom.

DEVO 9

WISDOM'S BLUEPRINTS

The Lord laid the earth's foundations
with wisdom's blueprints.
—PROVERBS 3:19

And the Living Expression was with God . . . .
And through his creative inspiration
this Living Expression made all things,
for nothing has existence apart from him!
—JOHN 1:1, 3

He is . . . God's true wisdom, and our Messiah.
—1 CORINTHIANS 1:24

READ: PROVERBS 3:19–20; JOHN 1:1–11

When you build a house or work on a construction site, you know there is always a blueprint drawn up by an architect. However, when it comes to the creation of the earth, the leading explanation in our culture is the Big Bang Theory. Because current instruments don't allow astronomers to peer back at the universe's birth, much of what is known comes from mathematical formulas and models. With this theory, there is no builder; there is no architect; there is no intelligent designer. Proverbs says otherwise. Here we learn that the builder is the Lord, and He is using Wisdom's blueprint. Who then is this Wisdom whose blueprint was followed to create our world? The mystery is solved in the book of John. It speaks of "the Living Expression," present in the beginning, through whose creative inspiration all things were brought into existence (John 1:5). Who then is this Living Expression? It's Jesus, the Son of God, the Light of Truth, the One John the Baptist prophesied would come to the very people He created.

CHALLENGE: Go back through Proverbs, and as you continue, wherever you see the word wisdom, if applicable, write "Jesus" instead. Note in your journal what you learn about Jesus from Proverbs. It will impact how you interact with Him.

DEVO 10

WISDOM, OUR HIDING PLACE

Never drift off course from these two goals for your life: to walk in wisdom and to discover discernment.
—PROVERBS 3:21

READ: PROVERBS 3:21–26

D id you ever attempt to drive with just one headlight? It can be terrifying, especially on a foggy night or in unfamiliar terrain. Your judgment is severely hampered. But with both headlights functioning, you can be at rest even in torrential rain storms or icy conditions. You are able to see ahead clearly, avoiding any hazards and making your way through.

If wisdom and discernment are like two headlights, what does each word mean? Biblical wisdom means knowing what's good for you and applying it. Biblical discernment is the ability to determine God's desire in a situation or identify the true nature of a circumstance. It appears that discernment needs to come first—discerning God's will so we then know how to apply it. How do we go about that? It comes from having a relationship with God, knowing Him, going deeper into the heart of Jesus. It will mean spending time with Him—meditating on Scripture not for head knowledge but for learning how very much the Lord loves us. In turn, we will come to love Him and desire only to do what pleases Him. And that is wisdom! For what pleases the Father will definitely be to our advantage, and by choosing His way, He will give us what it takes to accomplish it.

CHALLENGE: Take some time to dwell on wisdom and discernment by rereading Proverbs 3:22–26. Perhaps underline the benefits or even write them out in your journal. Then if you're faced with a decision, such as choosing a career, going back to school, joining some group, dating a particular person, or something as seemingly insignificant as watching a movie, take time to reread this devotion.

GOING DEEPER: Watch Discernment for Dummies, Parts 1 and 2, on YouTube.[7]

WISDOM IN RELATIONSHIPS

Every violent thug is despised by the Lord,
but every tender lover finds friendship with God
and will hear his intimate secrets.
—PROVERBS 3:32

READ: PROVERBS 3:27–35

Have you ever been guilty of not paying your debts and saying, "Sorry buddy, can't pay you today," when in reality you've got the money in your pocket?

Have you ever been guilty of saying to a friend who asks a favor, "Wish I could," when in fact you do have the resources at hand?

Have you ever been guilty of bullying under the guise of teasing? You say, "I was just joking! Can't you take a joke?"

Do you want to enjoy glory and honor, grace and favor, walk under a stream of God's blessings, or be considered a "thug" (v. 32)? Thug! Isn't that a bit overreactive to someone's words not being on par? But look at it as if you are the one who is the brunt of inconsideration or bullying. Would you not want God to serve justice? And He will, for God despises the inconsiderate and the bullies. On the other hand, those who do right by their neighbor are privileged to bask in the friendship of God Himself. They receive the honor of hearing His intimate secrets. Imagine: God being your friend, hanging out with Him and Him sharing with you what's on His heart—not just you telling Him what's on yours. So be wise; seek to do what is right.

CHALLENGE: Ask yourself the three questions posed at the beginning of this devo. Answer honestly. If you are guilty, repent to the Lord. Then go to the one you brushed aside and tell the truth. Go to the one you bullied and apologize. The fruit is friendship with God. Make a note of the date you took these actions and the outcome.

A FATHER'S INSTRUCTION

Wisdom is the most valuable commodity—so buy it! Revelation knowledge is what you need—so invest in it!
—PROVERBS 4:7

READ: PROVERBS 4:1–9

Investing in the stock market can be a risky business. Today up, tomorrow down. You've possibly studied the Great Crash of the U.S. stock market in 1929. Common folk like chauffeurs and cooks were borrowing money, mortgaging their homes, depleting their life savings to buy stocks that proved to be worthless on Black Tuesday, October 29. This paved the way for the Great Depression of the 1930s.

But there is a no-risk commodity: wisdom. With it you will reap the dividends of protection, honor, favor, beauty, and grace. "You will reign in life" (v. 4), be "victorious in the race" (v. 9). However, what's the cost? What must you invest? It's simple, yet not so simple: be an investor in Wisdom, in Jesus Himself Stock in Wisdom pays greater dividends than all the stocks in the world. For what value does earthly wealth hold if you do not know Jesus Christ? If you know Him, then do everything He says. Don't let His words "go in one ear and out the other" (v. 5).

CHALLENGE: Reread Proverbs 4:1–9 as if it were Jesus speaking to you. He says in Revelation 21:6–7, "I am . . . the beginning and the end. I will give water to all who are thirsty. As my gracious gift, they will continuously drink from the fountain of living water. . . . I will continue to be their God and they will continue being children for me." In what circumstance today could you use wisdom? Then invest time in drinking from the Fountain. You will receive the revelation knowledge you need. Record the fruit of this challenge.

TWO PATHWAYS

The lovers of God walk on the highway of light . . .
But the wicked walk in thick darkness.
—PROVERBS 4:18–19

READ: PROVERBS 4:10–19

If you haven't been hiking, by all means try it! Pick a balmy spring day or a crisp autumn one. Enjoy the heady scent of nature.

At the outset there are several trails usually marked in various colors by signs that describe the trails as being either easy, medium, or difficult. Say you choose the blue trail of medium difficulty. Some distance up (or down as in the case of the Grand Canyon) there is an unmarked fork in the path. Now what do you do? That depends on you. If you choose to continue on the blue trail, you can be certain of your destination. But the other fork, albeit it unmarked, looks more enticing and appeals to your adventurous nature, so you take it. Then a little warning light goes off in your brain, causing you to rethink your choice.

Experienced hikers will tell you: stick to your plan. Who knows what you might run into, like a mother bear and her cubs! Turning around is your best decision. This is Wisdom speaking. Receive her words no matter how hard they are to swallow or how much they irk your ego. They will "snap you back into place" and "be invigorating life to you" (v. 13).

CHALLENGE: Life is filled with many paths to choose from, and each path has its own set of challenges, some easier than others. Do some online research (for example, check out this link: https://www.nps.gov/grca/planyourvisit/index.htm) to discover what is involved in hiking the Grand Canyon. Apply what you learn to what it takes to navigate life! What lessons can you learn about making life choices by learning about hiking?

HEALING WORDS

Fill your thoughts with my words
until they penetrate deep into your spirit.
—PROVERBS 4:21

READ: PROVERBS 4:20–24

I f you're like most young adults, you undoubtedly planned some time this week to go to the gym or meet up with friends for a hike or a game of basketball. Physical exercise is a big priority for all adults; it's a good foundation for being fit in old age.

According to Solomon, words are also important—actually even more important. Why is this so? Why is it that he warns us to "above all, guard the affections of your heart" (v. 23)? Because words indeed "penetrate deep into your spirit" (v. 21) and can impact "the welfare of your innermost being" (v. 23). In fact, Proverbs 18:21 states it emphatically: "Your words are so powerful that they will kill or give life."

Jesus also taught something similar: "What comes out of your mouth reveals the core of your heart. Words can pollute" (Matthew

15:18). Negative, ungodly words pollute our thought life and thus our actions. The apostle Paul exhorts us to "capture, like prisoners of war, every thought and insist that it bow in obedience to the Anointed One" (2 Corinthians 10:5). If words are indeed this powerful, should we not be more aware of what we listen to and what we read? Most importantly, we need to fill our hearts with His words.

CHALLENGE: Take inventory of the condition of your heart. Just as we know the importance of conditioning our hearts aerobically for good health, so should we focus on the conditioning of our heart spiritually. Where is your focus, the physical or the spiritual? Answer honestly, and then make any necessary changes in what you are currently listening to and reading.

WATCH WHERE YOU'RE GOING

Set your gaze on the path before you. With fixed purpose, looking straight ahead, ignore life's distractions.
—PROVERBS 4:25

READ: PROVERBS 4:25–27

D o you remember your days in Little League when the coach, even the fans, shouted, "Keep your eye on the ball"? When at bat, if you looked elsewhere or let distractions sidetrack you, you would swing and miss and hang your head in shame. But when you kept your gaze fixed, intent on hitting the ball, you'd hear the crack of the bat and the roar of the crowd.

The Lord is our coach reminding us from the sidelines to keep our focus on the path before us—the one that "has been already marked out . . . look away from the natural realm and . . . fasten [your] gaze onto [Me]" (Hebrews 12:1–2). "Then [you'll] be able to run life's marathon race with passion and determination" (Hebrews 12:1).

CHALLENGE: You're running life's marathon. All runners on the racetrack run to win, but "only one receives the victor's prize" (1 Corinthians 9:24). If we are on the right path, the one marked out for us by the Lord, we will win—if we run with the intent to be victorious! So first check in with the Coach and be sure you're on the right track, in the right lane. Make any needed corrections, and run with all your heart.

AVOID PROMISCUITY

*Listen to me, my son . . . Listen carefully to my advice
so that wisdom and discernment will enter your heart.*
—PROVERBS 5:1–2

READ: PROVERBS 5:1–14

Picture this scenario: there's a guy or gal you're friendly with from work, from class, from the gym, from church, or elsewhere, who sends the occasional flirty text or gives the knowing smile as you chat. Do you find yourself drawn into these conversations, enticed by the romantic undertones?

Or maybe you have discovered a website that seduces you into late evenings online. Do you find yourself so longing for more that you're quieting the voice of the Holy Spirit when He shouts, "Flee"? Hear the cry of your Father as He pleads, "Run away . . . as fast as you can" (v. 7). A cruel fate awaits you. Change your routine, change your schedule, confide in a friend that a "certain someone," whether in the flesh or on the screen, is causing you untoward distress. Take whatever action needed. Remember, Satan wants more than anything to ruin your life, and sexual temptation is one of the most common ways he works. Succumbing to this temptation will cost you.

This is not just Christianese. Secular psychologists also point out the dire consequences of promiscuity and pornography, including depression and anxiety as well as lowered self-esteem.[8] There is more to it than just unwanted pregnancies and sexually transmitted diseases and abhorrent sexual appetites.

Then there is the ultimate consequence: God's judgment. Is this, indeed, the road you want to choose?

CHALLENGE: Go back and check out Devo 5. There, too, Solomon was talking about the seductress, but here he seems even more concerned, as if his son hadn't really listened to him before. What about you? Are you being tempted by the seducer/seductress? Are you yourself being seductive? If you are in any way guilty, then follow the directions given in the Devo 5 challenge. It will put you back on the right road.

GOING DEEPER: It is also helpful to tell someone about your struggle and your decision to cut off communication with the "seductress" (v. 3). Ask them to keep you accountable. Sin loses its power when it is brought into the light. As James states, "confess your sins to one another, and pray for one another so that you may be healed" of your struggle (James 5:16 NASB).

SEX RESERVED FOR MARRIAGE

My son, share your love with your wife alone.
Drink from her well of pleasure and from no other.
—PROVERBS 5:15

READ: PROVERBS 5:15–23

Once again, we hear a father pleading with his son. Solomon knew from bitter experience—a man with seven hundred wives and three hundred concubines (see 1 Kings 11:3 if you don't believe it)—that sharing his love with more than one woman robbed him of his destiny. Continue reading 1 Kings 11 and you'll discover that Solomon's actions led to his downfall. In attempting to win favor with his wives, he fell out of favor with God. The kingdom of Israel, which was initially given to Solomon, was torn from the hands of his son Rehoboam. Only the tribe of Judah was left to his bloodline because of God's promise to David,

Solomon's father.

Headlines today in the post-Christian era support these scriptures. Famous movie producers, Olympic coaches, CEOs, church leaders, Catholic priests, and presidents have lost status, even served prison time, for their inappropriate sexual conduct. The father in Proverbs 5 begs his son not to take this road. The fruit is a seared conscience and lack of self-control, leaving you a captive to sex and robbed of your destiny.

CHALLENGE: Since this devotional is meant for single young adults, these words are to be read as a mind-set for right now as well as for when you may marry. Solomon had everything a man could want, including any woman, but he was never satisfied (check out Ecclesiastes, which Solomon also wrote). Multiple spouses, lovers, affairs do not satisfy. Having one spouse does. So, write out a covenant to reserve the pleasure of sex for your future spouse—after you're married!

GOING DEEPER: Perhaps you are currently dating your future spouse and you're wondering, Is sex okay? Can we live together before we say, "I do"? Wouldn't it be a good idea to test-drive the car before we buy it? Not according to the title of this passage: "Sex Reserved for Marriage." Despite the prevalence of sex outside marriage in our culture, social scientists have discovered that couples who cohabit are 30 to 80 percent more likely to divorce, are more vulnerable to sexual infidelity, and struggle with more unhappiness.[9] If you are in this predicament, move out—today. Trust God to show you how or if you are to continue the relationship. He does not want you robbed of your destiny.

DEVO 18

WORDS OF WISDOM

If you cosign a loan for an acquaintance . . .
quickly get out of it if you possibly can!
—PROVERBS 6:1, 3

READ: PROVERBS 6:1–5

A mong the first congratulations you receive for your eighteenth birthday is "You now qualify for a credit card." You sign up and begin to build a reputation as a person of your word. But stuff happens and you get behind. Or you're careless and overspend. The credit card company starts breathing down your neck. You check out other sources to borrow the money to pay it off, but your credit rating requires someone to cosign for you.

Now consider this circumstance in reverse. Suppose it's your friend in financial straits, and he persuades you to cosign for him. But what if they default? You become responsible for your friend's irresponsibility. Solomon suggests that before that happens you get out of the agreement. Wouldn't that mean going back on your agreement to cosign? However, even Jesus warned us not to bind ourselves by taking an oath at all, and that includes cosigning a loan (see Matthew 5:33–37).

Do you understand the seriousness of such an agreement? You will have to pay up if your "friend" drops the ball. You need to be prepared to bear the full weight of the repayment no matter the reasons your friend couldn't do so.

CHALLENGE: If you have cosigned for someone and do not have the means to pay if they should default, then "swallow your pride . . . and go tell your 'friend' you want your name off that contract. . . . You'll be so relieved you did!" (v. 3, 5). On the other hand, if you have asked someone else to cosign for you, face the music and release them from your agreement. Choose to be solely responsible for your debts. Don't be embarrassed to seek counsel, if needed, on how to do it.

LIFE LESSONS

When you're feeling lazy, come and learn a lesson from this tale of the tiny ant.
—PROVERBS 6:6

READ: PROVERBS 6:6–15

The alarm is buzzing, playing some tune; it's time to get up for class, for work. You groan and hit the snooze button. Despite your body's complaints, you roll out of bed in time. The effort you put into your term paper pays off. You receive a promotion at the job for the innovation you submitted.

However, that's not always the case, right? Sometimes you decide to skip class or show up late for work. You let some chores slide, put off others till tomorrow. You stayed out late with friends. You were studying till three in the morning. You're tired, so you say to yourself, I'll just sit back awhile and take it easy.

Have you ever considered there could be a root cause for your seeming laziness when you were wanting to sleep in? Well, some years ago when you became a teen, a growth surge began and you actually did need more sleep—nine to ten hours, in fact! If twenty-one days can supposedly form a habit (research says it takes more like 254), it's easy to see why by the time you're eighteen when the growth surge is generally over—2,555 days later—sleeping in is your normal.[10]

But don't let this lead to poor decisions. Solomon warns that "by making excuses you'll learn what it means to go without" (v. 11). So he encourages us to learn from the ant. They not only prepare for today but also for tomorrow. Hopefully, you're among the industrious and are already reaping the benefits of your labor. Then you need never fear that "poverty will . . . move in as your roommate for life" (v. 11).

CHALLENGE: There are two arenas to consider: time management and financial management. Take stock of how you're doing. Is "laziness" contributing to mismanagement of your time or your finances? If yes, determine how you can rectify this. If you're not certain how, don't be embarrassed to seek counsel. Follow the example of the ant and enter into wisdom.

SEVEN THINGS GOD HATES

Putting others down while considering yourself
superior, spreading lies and rumors,
spilling the blood of the innocent,
plotting evil in your heart toward another,
gloating over doing what's plainly wrong,
spouting lies in false testimony, and
stirring up strife between friends.
These are entirely despicable to God!
—PROVERBS 6:17–19

READ: PROVERBS 6:16–23

This is one time you and Solomon—actually you and the Lord—will most likely totally agree. Who really likes an arrogant show-off or someone who makes fun of the innocent? You will quickly terminate a friendship that attempts to stir up strife between you and your other friends by spreading lies and rumors.

On the other hand, it's easy to give false testimony when you need a cover-up. What do a few white lies matter? As long as you only plot evil in your heart and don't take action, no harm is done. But these are evils God truly hates. They are an abomination to Him—"entirely despicable"! (v. 19). So, let this truth (that these are behaviors God hates) be "a bright beam of light shining into every area of your life, instructing and correcting you to discover the ways to godly living" (v. 23).

Where you have been haughty, you'll be humble. You will no longer bully but encourage the innocent. In the past, you stirred up strife, but now you promote unity. You are done with lies and rumors; instead, you stick with the truth. That includes not giving false testimony. As for plotting evil in your heart, you plan what's beneficial, a blessing for others. This wisdom will "guide you wherever you go and keep you from bringing harm to yourself . . . and direct you through a brand-new day" (v. 22).

CHALLENGE: Check out the list of evils above. There are seven. Search your heart, and if you find you're guilty of any of them, repent. Make amends where needed. Consider the suggestions given in the concluding paragraph of the devotion. If there's any hesitancy to take such actions, ask the Lord to reveal why you are hesitant.

GOING DEEPER: How do we go about changing our behavior? By surrendering our lives to Christ. If you haven't made Jesus Lord of your life, why not today? Ask a follower of Jesus to tell you how.

TRUTH OR CONSEQUENCES

Truth will protect you from immorality . . . '
For how can a man light his pants on fire
and not be burned?
—PROVERBS 6:25, 27

READ: PROVERBS 6:24–35

B ack when your great grandparents were kids, the game show Truth or Consequences was part of the evening entertainment. Contestants, who were selected from the studio audience, could either tell the truth (answer a question) or be forced to pay the consequences (perform a stunt). In most cases, people would answer incorrectly on purpose in order to subject themselves to the consequence. It made for good television.

However, entertainment is not life. In this reading from Proverbs, the subject is the consequence of adultery. Not good! Adultery isn't just related to a physical affair with another, but it's also a matter of affections being directed to someone other than your spouse.

But you might say, "I'm single. How does this apply to me?" So, let's look at it from a different angle. What about spiritual adultery? Are your affections being drawn away from God? Who or what is constantly on your mind, gets most of your attention, determines your every move? Is it your job, your course work, your girlfriend or boyfriend? Who or what can you not live without? Coffee in the morning, going to the gym, seeing that special someone? Where or to whom do you usually turn for advice, wisdom, help? Your best friend, your parents, your advisor, the internet?

You may not think of these things as "hot coals of fire" that can "blister [your] feet," but in reality, the wrong god can indeed destroy your life (v. 28). Why? God created us for Himself. He wants our full attention and devotion—like any husband would. Yet, the fury of God's jealousy is far greater than that of a man. Check out this portion of the Ten Commandments: "You shall have no other gods before me. . . . for I . . . am a jealous God, punishing the children for the sin of the parents to the third and fourth generation" (Exodus 20:3, 5 NIV). Wow! None of us want this. However, if we walk in God's truth, we will be protected from immorality—from serving lesser gods—and the Lord will show kindness to thousands of generations of our children (Exodus 20:6).

CHALLENGE: Answer honestly the questions posed in the devo above. Who or what is constantly on your mind, gets most of your attention, determines your every move? Who or what can you not live without? Where or to whom do you usually turn for advice, wisdom, help? Bottom-line, the question is this: who is your god?

WISDOM, YOUR TRUE LOVE

Say to wisdom, "I love you," and to understanding,
"You're my sweetheart."
"May the two of you protect me,
and may we never be apart."
For they will keep you from the adulteress,
with her smooth words meant to seduce your heart.
—PROVERBS 7:4–5

READ: PROVERBS 7

Some of you may already do ministry in the church as Sunday school teachers, youth group leaders, or worship team leaders. Some of you may actually be serving as youth pastors or even being groomed for the pulpit. Perhaps you're drawn to doing evangelistic campaigns on your campus or in your city or in a foreign field. How could there be any danger in that?

But Jesus gives a very serious warning in Matthew 7:21: "Not everyone who says to me, 'Lord, Lord,' will enter into the realm of heaven's kingdom." Yes, you may be doing good works in His name, but what is your motive? Is it His glory or your glory that you seek? The first commandment is not to do good works but to love the Lord "with every passion of your heart, with all the energy of your being, and with every thought that is within you" (Matthew 22:37). "But I do," you say. Are you sure? See John 14:23–24.

If you truly love Him, you'll obey His Word, not the board of some denomination or the precepts of some theological seminary. That means, not only will your motives be pure, you will not be caught pilfering money from the tithe box, hence serving a prison term, or visiting prostitutes and being defrocked or exposed for sexual abuse. "Your enemy, the devil, roams around incessantly, . . . looking for its prey to devour" (1 Peter 5:8), especially the young man or woman in service to the Lord. Beware! May you never abandon "the passionate love you had for [the Lord] at the beginning" (Revelation 2:4).

CHALLENGE: Whether we are in ministry or not, we are all charged to live life in a manner worthy of the Lord. Read these passages and select one to copy; then post it where you will see it daily: Ephesians 4:1; Philippians 1:27; Colossians 1:10; 1 Thessalonians 2:12.

WISDOM CALLING

"I'm calling to you, sons of Adam, yes, and to you
daughters as well. Listen to me
and you will be prudent and wise."
—PROVERBS 8:4–5

READ: PROVERBS 8:1–13

"Sons of Adam" and "daughters of Eve" (v. 4)—doesn't that remind you of royalty? That's God's destiny for you if you will listen to Wisdom's sermons. Everything she says is "unquestionably true" (v. 7), "clear and straightforward" (v. 9). Her words will empower you to "reign in life" (v. 6)!

But you might say, "I was always the class dummy"; "My sneakers were always the wrong brand"; "Nobody came to sit by me in the cafeteria." Now maybe the professors are suggesting you try another major, or your clothes are still the wrong brand, or no one is friendly to you at work. However, life is not defined by one's education or material things or even friendships. The Lord desires something more for you.

If you have an open mind, Wisdom will impart knowledge to you so that you discover there is something greater than being the descendant of Adam and Eve. Wisdom has "at [her] disposal living-understanding to devise a [new] plan for your life" so you can live as the son and daughter of the King (v. 12).

CHALLENGE: What is this "revelation-knowledge" that Wisdom desires to impart, and how do you attain it (v. 9–10)? Consider verse 13 and express your answer in words meaningful to you. Remember, in Devo 9, we learned that Wisdom can be seen as Jesus. What does today's passage reveal about how He desires to have input in your life?

THE POWER OF WISDOM

"You will find true success when you find me, for I have insight into wise plans that are designed just for you."
—PROVERBS 8:14

READ: PROVERBS 8:14–21

You are at a job interview, and to your happy surprise, the interviewer is trying to convince you that you are the best person for the position. Or perhaps you have been approached by a sports recruiter to attend a certain college. The recruiter promises not only a scholarship but the possibility of being scouted by the pros. Or you visit a car lot, where the salesman is eager to make a sale for the day. He'll even give you money for your old car.

In each scenario, you are being wooed—hopefully with your best interest in mind but likely with the motive that your contribution at the job, on the field, in the lot will generate revenue.

Check out what is being offered. You will not find a better job, a better college, a better deal. Wisdom is doing the same in these verses—offering you a better deal.

However, just as with the job, the college, and the car, Wisdom has expectations. So, what is expected of you with Wisdom's offer? It's neither performance nor finances. Wisdom's expectation is that you "love Me"—"passionately love Me" (v. 17). The halfhearted will not find Jesus.

CHALLENGE: Reread these verses and make note of what Wisdom has to offer. Is it worth the search? Will you "search and search continually" (v. 17)?

WISDOM IN THE BEGINNING

"I was there, close to the Creator's side,
as his master artist.
Daily he was filled with delight in me
as I playfully rejoiced before him.
I laughed and played, so happy with what he had
made."
—PROVERBS 8:30–31

READ: PROVERBS 8:22–31

Y ou dream of flying—no, not in a plane but tumbling in space, leaping from cloud to cloud, dancing on the moon. Looking down, you see that little blue marble teeming with life. A voice calls, "Come and play." Your ears perk up; who could that be? Then you remember—aha, it's Wisdom. Wisdom, God's Master Artist! Wisdom, which was before we were. Not something far off that we must strain to apprehend but at hand, calling for us, running to us, delighting in us. Wisdom that the

Father lavishes upon us. Wisdom that has always been and always will be. It will not change with the times nor disappear.

Yes, Wisdom is the Master Artist, and you are His creation. You are the fulfillment of all He longs for. You are the reason He was willing to die on a cross, making it possible for you and Him to laugh and play together, both now and in eternity (see Hebrews 12:2). Your heart somersaults with joy (see Psalm 16:11).

CHALLENGE: This joy is not just meant for eternity. It is meant for now as a Christ follower—in whatever your circumstances, good or bad. If that is not your experience, seek the Lord for why and follow His instructions.

WISDOM WORTH WAITING FOR

"If you wait at wisdom's doorway, longing to hear a word for every day, joy will break forth within you."
—PROVERBS 8:34

READ: PROVERBS 8:32–36

aiting! Waiting in line for the theater doors to open, for the drawbridge to close, for your turn to check out at the store. Waiting to get your test back, to find out if you made the team, to hear from your friend. Waiting—not your favorite thing to do, but if the payoff is worth it, you will hang in there. However, here the charge is to "wait at wisdom's doorway," to sit at Jesus' feet listening for the Holy Spirit to speak. You need a word of counsel? He is the counselor. Need instruction? He is the teacher. And the payoff? There's joy in His presence—pure bliss when you are face-to-face with Him (Psalm 16:11). You "will experience divine strength . . . , run . . . without growing weary, and walk through life without giving up" (Isaiah 40:31). The fountain of life will pour over you, and you will grow in the delight and favor of the Lord. Indeed, His "joy will break forth in you" (v. 34).

CHALLENGE: Set aside time each day, an hour, a half hour, even fifteen minutes, to "wait at wisdom's doorway" (v. 34). By all means, do what the Lord tells you each day. To ignore Him is to flirt with death.

GOING DEEPER: Experiment with the Lord's prayer (Matthew 6:9–13) as a model for waiting on the Lord: open with worship; then seek His plans for your day; take time to read His Word as well as make any requests you have; confess any known sins and forgive those who have wronged you; cry out for His rescue in trials and from attacks of the evil one; then close by acknowledging that He is "the King who rules with power and glory forever" (Matthew 6:13).

WISDOM'S FEAST

Wisdom . . . has made ready a banquet feast. . . .
She has sent out her maidens, . . .
inviting everyone to come.
—PROVERBS 9:1–3

READ: PROVERBS 9:1–12

The bride and the groom are now Mr. and Mrs., and you head to the wedding reception. You are still amazed that you were invited—then you learn everyone was! Hmm . . . As you sample the mouth-watering hors d'oeuvres and the delicately scented wine, and mingle with the other guests, your concerns are brushed aside. However, when you pick up your seating assignment, you discover there are only four tables. They are labeled the accusing cynic, the evil one, the mocker, and the wise. The guests seated at the first three tables look dark and angry, hurling hateful insults at the hosts. Furthermore, they have no wedding favors!

However, at each place on the table for the wise is a golden bell embossed with the date, and in the center is an elaborately embellished promise box. Guests reach into it and exclaim with delight as they draw out a miniature pillar inscribed with one of the seven qualities of wisdom: pure, peaceable, considerate, teachable, filled with love, never prejudiced or hypocritical, righteous! (see Proverbs 9:1 and James 3:17–18). How, you ask yourself, can I get assigned to that table? Is there something I need to do? Someone I need to speak to?

CHALLENGE: Reread the scripture passage to determine what is required to sit at Wisdom's table. There is one verse that makes it clear—one decision that will make every year of your life more fruitful than the one before. Which verse is it? Clue: look for the words "acquiring wisdom" (v. 10). Write it out in your own words.

GOING DEEPER: What do you think is the Lord's love language? Check your answer with John 14:23. Then ask yourself, Do I qualify to sit at Wisdom's table?

A SPIRIT NAMED FOOLISH

She's seductive and restless. . . . She preaches to all who walk by her who are clueless as to what is happening: "Come home with me."
—PROVERBS 9:13, 15–16

READ: PROVERBS 9:13–18

Sitting cross-legged, jackets tugged tight, we fellows watched the camp fire spiral upward. The flames curled, spitting out occasional bursts, lighting up our faces: three men and a woman. The woman had invited us earlier to join her on this campout. It seemed like a cool idea, so we grabbed our camping gear and climbed the trail, trudging up the long ascent. We helped her set up her tent, then set up our own. After a supper of sandwiches and coffee brewed over the fire, the evening stars began to appear. The scent of wood smoke and pine trees lulled our senses; we would have no problem sleeping no matter how hard the ground.

Here we were, clueless as to what was in store. Suddenly the woman laughed boisterously, jolting us from our reverie. She sent a knowing glance to each of us. "It'll be our little secret," she whispered sensuously as she crooked her finger in my direction, instantly igniting me. Then I noticed her eyes. My heart froze. Death—the spirit of death—stared back at me!

CHALLENGE: When faced with temptation, what should you do? Look up 1 Corinthians 6:18, 2 Timothy 2:22, James 4:7. Consider memorizing at least one of these verses, and be sure to use it when you're tempted in any way, not just sexually.

A FATHER REJOICES

When wisdom comes to a son, joy comes to a father.
—PROVERBS 10:1

READ: PROVERBS 10

Do you have a heart's desire to be a lover of God? Or is the draw of the world too enticing? Is God asking too much to love Him with "every passion of your heart, with all the energy of your being, and with every thought that is within you" (Matthew 22:37)? How is it possible, you ask, to love Someone you've never seen when you have difficulty loving those you have?

However, did you notice there are rewards for being a lover of God—even if you love Him imperfectly? You can "never be greatly shaken" (v. 30) because you "have a secure anchor" (v. 25). You are "enriched beyond belief" (v. 6) and thus enjoy a "feast of gladness" (v. 28). Others learn from you, and your "teachings . . . are like living truth flowing from the fountain of life" (v. 11). What more could you desire?

The greatest reward of all is you bring joy to your heavenly Father! The one who gave His only Son to prove His love for you is delighted that you love Him in return.

CHALLENGE: To what degree do you see yourself as a lover of God? How would you describe your relationship to Him? Would you like it to be more? Seek the Holy Spirit for answers—no leaning on your own opinions (Proverbs 3:5).

A MOTHER GRIEVES

When a son turns from wisdom, a mother grieves.
—PROVERBS 10:1

REREAD: PROVERBS 10

You sit in a prison cell gazing at a photo of your mom holding you as a toddler. Then there's the picture of you graduating from kindergarten standing between your proud parents. And in the last one, you're up to bat in a Little League game smartly dressed in your team's uniform.

But then came middle school! Life had a different look, you began skipping school, passing time at the local hangouts, awkwardly flirting with girls. Words of wisdom from your parents and teachers were like "rods beating [your] backside" (v. 13). High school only intensified these behaviors, and there was no going to college. The streets beckoned. You acquired your first gun.

Now you are sitting in prison marking off the days, yearning to taste your mother's cooking. The hope of an early release for good behavior is continually reeling through your thoughts. Visits with your mom are painful; your father doesn't bother.

That's your earthly father; your heavenly Father, on the other hand, hasn't given up on you! He pursues you, graciously offering you the gift of faith. "Come unto Me and find peace—even if you don't get an early release."

CHALLENGE: Assuming this is not your circumstance, is there a possibility you have dabbled with or been tempted with unwise choices that could lead to devastating consequences? Will you take a stand and "capture, like prisoners of war, every thought and insist that it bow in obedience to the Anointed One" (2 Corinthians 10:5)? Go for it. In fact, write this verse out and post it where you can read it daily. Better yet, memorize it and post it in your heart.

DEVO 31

LIVING IN RIGHTEOUSNESS

Evil people may get a short-term gain, but to sow seeds of righteousness will bring a true and lasting reward.
—PROVERBS 11:18

READ: PROVERBS 11

Who really defines what is right? Current culture indicates it's personal opinion. If it's good for me, then it's okay. And if it's not good for you, well . . . Someone drove by your parked car, knocked off your side view mirror, but never stopped to let you know. You're pregnant and your boyfriend says, "That's your problem." On the other hand, as you cash out a customer, you miscount the change, giving yourself a quarter here, a dime there. Rarely does a customer recount their change, so what does it hurt? The term paper you just handed in is mostly plagiarized, but who cares? The professor hardly has time to grade it, much less double-check your sources.

Do we really have to live righteously? Are there any benefits to living righteously? According to this chapter in Proverbs, living a life of righteousness benefits not only you but those around you as well, even an entire city (Proverbs 11:10–11). In the case of Nelson Mandela, his righteous behavior affected an entire nation! Raised Christian, he practiced the precepts of forgiveness and reconciliation that led to the downfall of apartheid in South Africa and his becoming South Africa's first democratically elected president. Both Mandela and his nation benefited from his righteous living.

Though you may not have the standing Nelson Mandela had, you could be the one writing the term paper, or cashing out a customer, or even getting your girlfriend pregnant; regardless of your circumstance, you can still choose to handle life righteously. It "will bring a true and lasting reward" in your life as well as in others' lives (v. 18).

CHALLENGE: Take time to go through Proverbs 11 and underline the benefits of righteous living—of being men and women of integrity. Then ask the Lord to reveal to you any ways in which you are not living righteously. Pray the prayer found in Psalm 19:13–14 and take action.

IT'S RIGHT TO LIVE FOR GOD

Hard work brings blessings back to you.
—PROVERBS 12:14

READ: PROVERBS 12:1–15

This chapter opens up with the idea of being teachable, and then thirteen verses follow sharing what we need to learn. The lessons apply to a variety of circumstances, some specific, like those of a wife (v. 4), an entrepreneur (v. 5), and a pet owner (v. 10), while others apply to us all. One concept, however, is repeated three times (vv. 9, 11, 14), and it focuses on working hard.

Verse 9 explains how we struggle with our identity, so we cover up with pretense. We gals make sure our outfits are coordinated, our makeup perfect. The guys buy a brand-new Jeep Wrangler rather than a used one and frequent uptown bars buying drinks all around. But that only drains away finances and incurs credit card debt. In the second instance, verse 11, the writer discusses the fact we chase pipe dreams, thinking that get-rich-quick schemes or playing the lottery or fantasy games will put food on the table. However, Solomon says, "work hard for a living" (v. 9), "work hard at your job" (v. 11), and you will have all that you need. Indeed, "put your heart and soul into every activity you do, as though you are doing it for the Lord Himself . . . For we know that we will receive a reward" (Colossians 3:23–24). Living for God frees us from pretense and pipe dreams. And the reward? We begin to find our identity in Christ, which is always much better than the pipe dream, and enjoy His provision and purpose for our lives.

CHALLENGE: Reread Proverbs 12:2–14 and select the life lesson that applies to you. Then ask the Lord to reveal how He would have you respond. Write it down, and make every effort to follow His instruction. Be teachable.

DEVO 33

WISDOM MEANS BEING TEACHABLE

To learn the truth you must long to be teachable,
or you can despise correction and remain ignorant.
—PROVERBS 12:1

READ: PROVERBS 12:1–15

You may wonder why you are reading the same portion of Scripture as you did in Devo 32. It's because this concept of being teachable, in verses 1 and 15, brackets the other verses. This is one trait, whether you're selling stocks or selling cars or selling hamburgers, that will always work in your favor, especially if your goal is leadership, i.e., to be a broker at the brokerage firm or the owner of the car dealership or the franchise owner of the hamburger joint. In each case, you'll want to listen before you speak. You can learn from your superiors, and you can also learn from your clientele.

In fact, every day through our entire lives we face multiple opportunities to exercise a teachable spirit rather than live in staunch, prideful ignorance. The difference lies in how we respond to the discipline of wisdom. Do you submit and listen with an open heart, or do you choose to reject wisdom from others and remain "in love with [your] own opinion" (v. 15)?

An open heart is key. "Those who listen with open hearts will receive more revelation. But those who don't listen with open hearts will lose what little they think they have!" (Mark 4:25). An "open heart" means you "listen well to wise counsel" and are "willing to learn from correction" (Proverbs 19:20). The choice is between "poverty and disgrace" or "honor" (Proverbs 13:18).

CHALLENGE: How do we obtain a teachable spirit? Try this prayer: "Lord, direct me throughout my journey so I can experience your plans for my life. Reveal the life-paths that are pleasing to you. Escort me along the way; take me by the hand and teach me" (Psalm 25:4–5). And take time to read this article: "True Leaders Are Teachable."[11]

LEARNING TO SPEAK WISELY

Reckless words are like the thrusts of a sword, . . .
meant to stab and to hurt.
But the words of the wise soothe and heal.
—PROVERBS 12:18

READ: PROVERBS 12:16–28; JAMES 3:2–10

"Reckless words" are not only like "the thrusts of a sword" (Proverbs 12:18), but they are also like a "small flame" (James 3:5). Think of the almost yearly wildfires in California that reduce millions of acres to ash, steal homes, take lives, and destroy all the life their flames can lick up.

So it is with our words, whether spoken innocently, foolishly, or even purposefully. They can release "a fire that can burn throughout the course of human existence" (James 3:6). Critical words spoken to children can become subconscious messages guiding their lives to destruction. Harsh words spoken to friends can make reconciliation inconceivable. Worst still, "if someone believes they have a relationship with God but fails to guard his words then his heart is drifting away and his religion [his devotion to God] is shallow and empty" (James 1:26).

The wiser course is to bridle the tongue and choose words that soothe and heal—words that encourage and restore joy to the heart. Be intentional, intentionally wise, with your words and enjoy the fruit of it. It's a matter of life and death.

CHALLENGE: Reread Proverbs 12, then go back and read Proverbs 10. Mark the verses that discuss the tongue. Ask the Holy Spirit to reveal where you need to change, and then examine your heart. "For what has been stored up in your hearts will be heard in the overflow of your words!" (Matthew 12:34). Begin today to make the needed changes.

LIVING WISELY

If you want to grow in wisdom, spend time with the wise.
—PROVERBS 13:20

READ: PROVERBS 13

"The wise" (v. 2)—whom do you consider to be "the wise"? If you've been working your way through these devotions, you've heard more than once: "the wise" are not always your buds or your besties, they're not necessarily your professors, and they're definitely not those on social media. By all means you don't want to be spending time with gossips who will probably in turn stab you in the back. (And God forbid that you should be the gossip! See Proverbs 13:3.) No! You want to choose the wise to look to as role models.

Who then is wise among your associates, your managers, your CEOs? According to Proverbs 13, it's those who "hate what is phony and false" (v. 5), who "shine brightly in darkness" (v. 9), who are "lovers of God" (v. 14). These are the wise to whom you should turn. Their wisdom comes from the "source of revelation-knowledge" which is none other than the Word of God, the Bible (v. 16).

Then there is the Wise One. Several of these devotions have pointed you to Jesus as the ultimate Wisdom. He is the one best qualified to spend time with!

CHALLENGE: Consider with whom you are spending time. What is the main attraction? Do they meet the qualifications given here? If there are any red lights, reconsider.

THE HOUSE OF WISDOM

A nation is exalted by the righteousness of its people,
but sin heaps disgrace upon the land.
—PROVERBS 14:34

READ: PROVERBS 14

What memories do you have of 2020? The pandemic was worldwide; you undoubtedly felt its effects in some way. Lost your job? Worked from home? Wore those masks that fogged up your glasses but you knew protected the other person? Socially distanced? Attended church on Zoom? Wondered if COVID-19 would ever end? Perhaps actually had the coronavirus!

Did you ask why? Why a pandemic, Lord?

Proverbs 14:34 perhaps gives a clue. We are not exactly a righteous nation. It's more than this being a post-Christian era; we are slipping into a Godless era. The living God is being replaced by lesser gods: the god of materialism fueled by the god of greed; the god of self or "us four and no more" with little thought to "love thy neighbor"; the god of power that corrupts, morphing into "absolute power [that] corrupts absolutely."[12] Biblical values have been disappearing for decades, and in 2020, it seems our sin heaped upon us God's displeasure.

How then can we, who are part of this nation, escape God's displeasure? In some regards, we cannot. But if in the circumstances, we choose to be "lovers of God who live in awe of him," we provide for ourselves and our children "a place of shelter and security," empowered "to escape death's domain" (Proverbs 14:26–27).

CHALLENGE: Reread Proverbs 14 and underline the word fool, noting the fruit of being foolish: wickedness. Do the same for the word wise: being a lover of God. Do any of these scenarios prick your conscience? If yes, what steps do you need to take to rectify it? Go for it! Choose wisdom and build a house that "opens a fountain of life within you" (v. 27) and "receives promotion from the King" (v. 35)!

WISDOM FAR BETTER THAN WICKEDNESS

Respond gently when you are confronted and you'll defuse the rage of another. Responding with sharp, cutting words will only make it worse. Don't you know that being angry can ruin the testimony of even the wisest of men? When wisdom speaks, understanding becomes attractive.
—PROVERBS 15:1–2

READ: PROVERBS 15:1–12

Your boss confronts you for an infraction you didn't commit. Will you react (i.e., act without thinking) or respond (i.e., think twice before taking action)? You know sharp cutting words will only make matters worse. So maybe you'll just quit the job; however, you need the paycheck.

An irate customer calls demanding that you, the customer service rep, provide restitution outside company policy. Will you react or respond? Will you sneer back, "No way!" or attempt to de-escalate the situation with reasonable words of empathy.

Yes, you know you should not react. But to respond will take wisdom—wisdom from above—and you can ask God for that (see James 1:5)! His wisdom "is always pure, filled with peace, considerate and teachable. It is filled with love and never displays prejudice or hypocrisy in any form and it always bears the beautiful harvest of righteousness!" (James 3:17–18).

CHALLENGE: Are you facing a similar circumstance? Describe. Then ask God for wisdom. Record what He tells you to do. Carry it out. What resulted? How did the Lord work in your heart?

THE EYES OF THE LORD

The eyes of the Lord are everywhere and
he takes note of everything that happens.
He watches over his lovers, and
he also sees the wickedness of the wicked.
—PROVERBS 15:3

READ: PROVERBS 15:1–12

Sometimes you engage in activities that if others knew, you'd be unfriended, fired! You know it's wrong, but since no one knows—at least no one here on Earth—you continue. Then you sense the piercing gaze of the Lord! Does that alarm you, or do you ignore Him?

There is a positive aspect to God's omniscience. He's not always "out to get you." He also watches over you. The Lord hears your sobs of loneliness, and suddenly a friend calls and says, "Let's go out, hanging, hiking, or hitting the stores." He is aware, even before you are, that you need a brake job that you can't afford.

Then you meet a guy at work who not only knows how to repair brakes but is willing to get his hands greasy at no cost. Your cat had kittens—too many! But all your friends want a fur ball! Yes, God even cares about kittens.

Are these just coincidences or God-incidences?

But suppose your circumstances are like Job's? You are a faithful lover of God, a servant He esteems. Then someone rams into your car from the rear, causing excruciating back pain. Flames race through your parents' home; your little sister does not escape. Does this mean God took His eye off you? As a follower of Jesus Christ, the enemy cannot touch you without the Lord's permission. His eye is on you—always.

CHALLENGE: Think back over your life. When have you known God's providential care or His discipline or had trials that came out of nowhere? What did you learn about Him from those circumstances? Put your thoughts in writing.

GOING DEEPER: Read Job's story, particularly chapters 1, 2, and 40–42. The Lord allowed Job to be severely tested, and though he questioned God, he still trusted him (Job 13:15). Would that be the case for you?

LIVING AN ASCENDED LIFE

The source of revelation-knowledge is found as you fall down in surrender before the Lord.
Don't expect to see Shekinah glory
until the Lord sees your sincere humility.
—PROVERBS 15:33

READ: PROVERBS 15:13–33

On any given day, someone may shout out at you, "Smile!" A big grin is easily returned when everything is going smoothly. But what about when, despite your best efforts, every day is a constant struggle and nothing seems to be working out? These proverbs, however, indicate there is something far more—like every day filled with joy and fullness not dependent on our earthly circumstances. It's a life that puts a real smile on your face! How do we receive that?

Proverbs 15:13 tells us that "a cheerful heart puts a smile on your face." That leads to the question: how do we attain such a heart?

77

In verse 15, we discover that to have such a heart is a choice. And verse 30 tells us that the choice is to "focus on what is beautiful." Okay, so what does that mean? The New Testament helps with an answer: "So keep your thoughts continually fixed on [i.e., focused on] all that is authentic and real, honorable and admirable, beautiful and respectful, pure and holy, merciful and kind" (Philippians 4:8). What could possibly live up to that criteria? It's not what; it's Who! None other than Jesus Christ! When we focus on Him, when we spend time in His presence, we are filled with joy (see Psalm 16:11).

CHALLENGE: How do you manage when life doesn't put a smile on your face? It depends on the choices you make. Choose to "focus on what is beautiful" (v. 15). Record what has been wrong in your life, how you can refocus, and what is the outcome when you do.

GOING DEEPER: This section of Proverbs is full of good advice on how to "Live an Ascended Life." For example, see verses 17, 19, 22, 24, 27, 28, 31. Select one and consider how you can implement into your life the wisdom given.

WISDOM EXALTS GOD

Within your heart you can make plans for your future, but the Lord chooses the steps you take to get there.
—PROVERBS 16:9

READ: PROVERBS 16:1–9

You are at that point in life where you make plans, set goals. You desire to be a veterinarian or get married or hike the Adirondack Trail. You may even have a plan to achieve your goal that you're continually scrutinizing, reevaluating. Each step seems critical, like a winning or losing chess move in the game of life. In the end, however, it will be the Lord who ultimately chooses if and how you'll arrive.

We may ask, Why have a goal, why make plans, if God has the overriding veto? Are we so "in love with our own opinions" that to put our "trust totally in God" seems foolish and absurd (vv. 2–3)? Such a mind-set is unwise. Better to let God have the final word; then, our plans reflect His desires, and we are guaranteed success. He will even turn our enemies into friends!

So, go ahead and set goals, make plans, but with this attitude: "Our tomorrows are in the Lord's hands and if he is willing we will . . . do this or that" (James 4:15).

CHALLENGE: Do you tend to make plans without any thought of submitting them to God? How do you react when your plans are thwarted? Reconsider your to-do list and place it in the Lord's hands. Let Him choose the steps you will take, and every plan you make will succeed. You "will live life to its fullest" (James 4:15).

LIVING LIKE A KING

Everyone wants gold, but wisdom's worth is
far greater. Silver is sought after, but a heart of
understanding yields a greater return.
—PROVERBS 16:16

READ: PROVERBS 16:10–20

"Living like a king"—what does that mean to you? Driving a Lexus? Having the latest iPhone? Time and money to check out all the restaurants in New York City or San Francisco or Chicago? Wearing the latest fashion with shoes to match each outfit? Earning top dollar as opposed to minimum wage? A plus at your new job being a 401K bonus?

Yes, everyone wants gold and silver, but if you reread verses 10–15, you'll have a different take. "Living like a king" means you'll have a place of standing in your community, among your peers, at your workplace. You'll set the standards as a CEO, as captain of your team, the big brother, and they will be righteous. No one will fault you for despising wrongdoing. All your employees, your team mates, your younger siblings will enjoy being in your presence and seek to please you.

The advice then for "living like a king" is to seek wisdom and a heart of understanding. The worth of wisdom is far greater than gold, the yield beyond that of silver.

CHALLENGE: Today's passage concludes with "one who trusts in God is blessed beyond belief!" (v. 20). Do you believe this? If yes, list the evidence for why. If no, list the evidence for why not. If you're of two opinions, explain. Whatever the case, ask the Lord for His input.

DEVO 42

WALKING WITH WISDOM

Nothing is more appealing than speaking beautiful, life-giving words. For they release sweetness to our souls and inner healing to our spirits [i.e., bones].
—PROVERBS 16:24

READ: PROVERBS 16:21–30; PROVERBS 4:20–24

A long time ago, a tiny red circle appeared on my arm. Each day, it increased in diameter. It seemed I was being eaten alive! I had no medical insurance, but my friend's doctor agreed to see me and gave me an ointment to apply three times a day. It seemed too simplistic to me, like being brushed off as a non-paying customer. I thought about getting a second opinion. But with no medical insurance, it was not an option.

Then our omniscient God reminded me: Scripture, stored in our hearts, becomes a wellspring of wisdom and understanding that we can draw from over and over. He quickened to memory that His words release prosperity to my soul and healing for my bones. Hadn't I also learned, if this is what God had provided—a freebie—why be too proud to receive it (Proverbs 16:18)? The doctor had told me to come in for a follow-up appointment, but I didn't need to; the condition was completely gone within three days!

"Life-giving words," when spoken to ourselves, when spoken to others, "release sweetness to our [or their] souls and inner healing to our [or their] spirits, i.e., bones" (v. 24). Be wise, be discerning, and speak in such a way as to be a fountain of life for others as well as yourself.

CHALLENGE: Watch a very short teaching video on YouTube by Derek Prince called "God's Medicine Bottle."[13] Write out the directions given, and try them out the next time you're dealing with an illness and have no medical insurance.

DEVO 43

WISDOM'S VIRTUES

Wise instruction is like a costly gem.
It turns the impossible into success.
—PROVERBS 17:8

READ: PROVERBS 17

In Proverbs 16:16, we were encouraged to pursue wisdom, to seek it with all our heart. Proverbs 17 give us some practical reasons why we should.

Are you feeling overwhelmed by the trials of life? Does your car shake, rattle, and roll, but it's your only mode of transport? Maybe your manager has it in for you, or your next-door neighbor is annoying, to say the least. Trials serve a purpose, according to Proverbs 17:3, calling them God's refining fire, which allows the impurities in our character to surface and be "skimmed off." The fruit comes when you begin to take on the character of Jesus. Now, that makes the trial worth your while (see Romans 8:28–29).

What about the friends in your life? Do they stand by you through thick and thin, as verse 17 talks about? Are they superficial, or do they truly love you? Will they speak the hard truth to you, even when it hurts to hear? "You can trust a friend who wounds you with his honesty" (Proverbs 27:6). That's the kind of friend to find. That's the kind of friend to be.

Then comes the mouth! Are you reactive or responsive? Verses 27 and 28 encourage us to bridle our tongue, in fact shut our mouths when we are provoked. Even if you are considered a fool, you'll look smart if you bite your tongue. No harm in looking smart!

Now that you've been given some reasons why you should pursue wisdom, be sure to complete the challenge below so you can discern which scenario above is significant to you.

CHALLENGE: Reread Proverbs 17, asking the Lord to point out a verse or two that you should seriously consider. What action should you take? Record what He says and make a plan to walk it out.

DEVO 44

WISDOM GIVES LIFE

The character of God is a tower of strength, for the lovers of God delight to run into his heart and be exalted on high.
—PROVERBS 18:10

READ: PROVERBS 18

Where do you run when trouble comes? Do you flee to earthbound remedies or run directly to God? How do you react at the first sign of hardship? Do you jump into the pit of despair or turn to the tower of strength? What do you do when a project or assignment seems too difficult to pursue? Do you just throw in the towel or seek God's counsel?

All too often, when the roommate moves out in a huff, our job is terminated, our favorite grandparent passes on, we tend to look either to ourselves or some form of painkiller before we cry out to God. Why not run to the Father? His character is unquestionable. He is "a tower of strength" (v. 10). He is able to lift us up in the midst of our dilemma, for He "has made us to be more than conquerors" (Romans 8:37). God can not only prevent us from falling into depression, help us avoid self-pity, and teach us to overcome hopelessness, but His love will also empower us to "triumph over death, life's troubles, fallen angels, or dark rulers in the heavens" (Romans 8:38). Don't procrastinate, "run into his heart and be exalted on high" (v. 10).

CHALLENGE: Turning to God is easier said than done. However, James 1:5 says you can ask God for His wisdom to be a conqueror. Take a difficulty that you are currently facing. Acknowledge that God has said you can conquer it, and then ask Him what you will need to do or not do. Journal this experience. In the future, don't let trials conquer you; remember, run with delight into the heart of the Father.

WISDOM EXALTED

*There are some people who ruin their own lives
and then blame it all on God.*
—PROVERBS 19:3

READ: PROVERBS 19:1–15

Humans have been playing the "blame game" since the beginning of time. Man blamed woman. The woman blamed Satan: "The devil made me do it!" We can add, as did her own flesh, that apple looked too delicious to resist. Plus, the serpent informed her she would become like God! Besides, God would overlook it. Wasn't He their friend who came to visit each evening?

But when evening came, God did not overlook it, the truth was uncovered, and Satan laughed! He had succeeded. Man's relationship with God had been destroyed. It would take the death of God's only Son, Jesus Christ, to create a path for the redemption of mankind and provide an opportunity for intimacy with God, the Father—to enjoy those walks in the garden with Him.

Don't let the blame game rule your life. Take the route of the wise. Recognize and take responsibility for your choices. Acknowledge that your misfortune is the fruit of your own doing and not God's. You will be forgiven. That is His promise: "if we freely admit our sins . . . he will be faithful to forgive us every time. God is just to forgive us our sins because of Christ, and he will continue to cleanse us from all unrighteousness" (1 John 1:9). Then you will once again experience the joy of His presence—of walking in the garden with Him.

CHALLENGE: Have you ever been guilty of playing the blame game? Describe the circumstance and ask yourself, "Who was really at fault?" Then ask God to reveal the truth.

GIVING GOD'S WAY

Every time you give to the poor
you make a loan to the Lord.
Don't worry—you'll be repaid in full.
—PROVERBS 19:17

READ: PROVERBS 19:16–29; MALACHI 3:8–10; 2 CORINTHIANS 9:5–11

When do I give to the poor? I do sometimes go through my closet and pass on clothes I no longer wear. I like to volunteer at the outreach dinners for the homeless. I also know some of my tithes are used to help out the poor.

One Sunday, the pastor shared from Malachi. The pastor challenged us, "Have you robbed God?" Could it be that "a loan to the Lord" was like a tithe (Proverbs 19:17)? "Are you tithing," the pastor questioned, "and are you tithing on the gross or just the net?"

I squirmed. Had I tithed on the gross that month, I wouldn't have had enough to pay my rent. That would've been poor stewardship. But Malachi also said the Lord would pour out a blessing beyond my comprehension. Nonetheless, I wasn't convinced.

A few days later, the Holy Spirit led me to 2 Corinthians 9:6: "Let giving flow from your heart, not from some sense of religious duty. Let it spring up freely from the joy of giving—all because God loves hilarious generosity!" And He will supply for your every need, plus more. This will be hilarious, I thought, but I'll give it a try. I'll tithe on the gross of my next paycheck.

Before my next paycheck, I received an unexpected gift of five hundred dollars—far more than the tithe! Then came the next month and my employer decided to pay me retroactively for my previous work experience. By this point I was convinced, and God had more than repaid me in full. You can't out give God.

CHALLENGE: Check your motives; are you a cheerful giver unto the Lord (Colossians 3:23), or are you giving with gritted teeth? Pray about it and take appropriate action.

ARE YOU LIVING WISELY?

It is the Lord who directs your life, for each step you take is ordained by God to bring you closer to your destiny. So much of your life, then, remains a mystery!
—PROVERBS 20:24

READ: PROVERBS 20

When I was in my twenties, I lived in Florida, and a young woman who had just moved there from Missouri needed housing. I had a one-bedroom apartment, and I did not want a roommate. But God had a destiny for me.

She moved in. After we became friends, she brought me to a Christian concert. I liked the band's music, and one song in particular grabbed my heart. I bought their record even though I didn't own a record player (this was before CDs.)

Eventually, my roommate decided to move back to Missouri. I had no particularly desire to remain in Florida, so I headed to Chapel Hill, North Carolina, to bunk down with my brother's family. My sister-in-law just so happened to be a former member of a sorority at UNC, and they needed a house mother! I took the job. Right across the street was the campus, so I decided to go for a master's degree. As God would have it, I not only got accepted but received a full scholarship—without even applying for it—which included a two-hundred-dollar monthly stipend! (I never used this degree professionally, but God had a destiny that could only have begun in North Carolina.)

In those days, I woke up to secular music on my clock radio. Three mornings in a row, Christian music rang in my ears! What is going on?! That's not my station! The first two mornings I switched it back to the secular station. But on the third morning, I kept listening and called the Christian station. I asked them to play my song, the one I'd had heard in Florida. They didn't have it, but when I said I had the record, they encouraged me to bring it in.

When I went to the radio station, all because of a song and God's mysterious maneuverings—which I thought were my decisions—my walk with the Lord radically changed. Through these new friends at the radio station, I discovered a church that believed in all the gifts of the Spirit, and soon after, I became a follower of Christ, not just a believer. I found my destiny.

CHALLENGE: All of these events took place in my life between the ages of twenty-eight and thirty-three, so it is very possible God is doing something similar with you—directing your steps without you having a clue it is actually Him. Take time to consider where you are and how you got there. Can you see His fingerprints?

GOD IS THE SOURCE OF WISDOM

It pleases God more when we demonstrate godliness and justice than when we merely offer him a sacrifice.
—PROVERBS 21:3

READ: PROVERBS 21

B uzz goes the alarm; you hit the floor and grab your Bible. Today's reading is three chapters in James, and you absolutely must pray. You hear your mom calling to come help get your siblings ready for school. You yell back, "Sorry, Mom. I've got to do ten more minutes with God."

You make it a habit to fast once a week for the unsaved on your campus. In fact, you think it's racking up brownie points with God. Then on one of those fast days, a new student in the dorm texts, "Let's go get a bite." What should you do?

What do you think Jesus would do? "There is something

more important to God than all the sacrifices and burnt offerings: it's the commandment to constantly love God with every passion of your heart . . . and to love your neighbor in the same way as you love yourself" (Mark 12:33). Where your mom is concerned, don't make up rules that exempt you from following God's word to honor your parents. She is as much your neighbor as the student in the dorm (Mark 7:10–13).

The prophet Micah perhaps explains this Proverb best: "With what shall I come to the Lord . . . Shall I come to Him with burnt offerings, with yearling calves? Does the Lord take delight in thousands of rams . . . ?" (Micah 6:6–7 NASB). No! What the Lord requires of you is "to do justice, to love kindness, and to walk humbly with your God" (Micah 6:8 NASB).

CHALLENGE: If you sense you don't measure up, that you have put religious duty above loving your neighbor, do not come under condemnation just begin to follow Micah's edict. In humility seek the Lord to help you treat your neighbor justly and kindly. He will give you the specifics; then follow through.

HOW TO LIVE A LIFE OF WISDOM

The rich and the poor have one thing in common: the Lord God created each one.
—PROVERBS 22:2

READ: PROVERBS 22:1–16

Y	ou earn minimum wage or a million plus. You're a blue-collar worker or white. Does it make a difference in man's eyes? Yes! What about in God's?

Ethnicity, language, social standing, gender, much less income bracket—none of these influence Him. Nor should they influence us. We are the pinnacle of God's creation—created in His image, inherently invaluable. His finger formed us in our mother's womb, each of us uniquely (Psalm 139:13). "Even before we were born, God planned in advance our destiny and the good works we would do to fulfill it!" (Ephesians 2:10). No matter what works the Lord has planned for us to do, we need to remember He is our maker, and that's what binds us together—not whether we are rich or poor.

Though income can determine where we live, what we eat, how we dress, it's no reason to hold another at arm's length. Distinctions that exist in life are abolished in death. What will it matter in eternity?

CHALLENGE: There is one distinction that matters in eternity: that is our relationship with Jesus Christ. We are all offered the opportunity to have eternal life (John 3:16). The steps we need to take are found in Acts 2:38. If you haven't done so, be wise and do so today! Lay "your life down in tender surrender before the Lord" and live life abundantly (Proverbs 22:4).

SAYINGS OF THE WISE SAGES

Pay attention to these excellent sayings . . .
For within my words you will discover true and
reliable revelation.
They will give you serenity so that you can reveal the
truth of the word of the one who sends you.
—PROVERBS 22:20–21

READ: PROVERBS 22:17–29

"Listen up," says the instructor. "You are headed out on a mission to represent the King and His kingdom. Your words must be an accurate representation, and your style of presentation must be flawless."

You query, "What must I do to prepare?"

Search the Scriptures. Meditate on the Word. Ask the Holy Spirit to guide you into all truth, for He only speaks what He hears from the King (John 16:13).

"Okay, I get that. But," you say, still puzzled, "where is it I'm being sent?"

The instructor smiles. "Didn't you learn that song when you were a kid in Sunday School? 'All around the neighborhood I'm gonna let it shine.'"

Um, maybe yes and maybe no. However, Scripture does say, "Your lives light up the world . . . . So don't hide your light! Let it shine brightly before others"—aha, that's the neighborhood!— "so that the commendable things you do will shine as light upon them, and then they will give their praise to your Father in heaven" (Matthew 5:14, 16). In this way, you will have given an accurate representation of the King.

"One more thing," the instructor adds. "Remember it is the King who is sending you out. You are not self-appointed, and He has given you what to say—words that result in eternal life, the purpose of your mission" (see John 12:49–50).

CHALLENGE: When was the last time you shared the gospel with someone? Are you prepared to share about the hope that is within you, to explain your faith to anyone who asks you? (1 Peter 3:15). As followers of Christ, we should obey His last words to us. And if you don't remember, it's okay. Just be sure to check them out in Matthew 28:18–20.

WISDOM WILL PROTECT YOU

Who has anguish? Who has bitter sorrow?
Who constantly complains and argues?
Who stumbles and falls and hurts himself?
Who's the one with bloodshot eyes?
—PROVERBS 23:29

READ: PROVERBS 23

You slowly sit up on the edge of your bed; your head pounds and your knee hurts from your fall when you stumbled out of the bar. How did you get here? Why? Were you looking for acceptance, trying to be cool? Attempting to escape unpaid bills, college debt, or the job you just lost? Are you lonely, away from home, looking for friends? The sneers of your classmates or your workmates doesn't let up; you fail one more time, and the alcohol takes away the pain.

You peer down at the scale. No wonder your jeans don't fit. But those donuts and especially the chicken alfredo with the noodles dripping in sauce, who could resist? Look around you, most others look just like you. Besides, pasta is cheaper than meat and veggies. So, what's the big deal, especially when each nibble helps take away the pain?

But where will it get you? Solomon warns that "drunkenness brings the sting of a serpent . . . spreading poison into your soul" (v. 32) and "gluttons sleep their lives away and end up broke!" (v. 21).

However, did you know: Jesus was accused of being a glutton and a drunkard?! (Luke 7:34). This friend of sinners died to provide forgiveness for all who lack self-control. You're not a hopeless cause. Listen to the Lord as His beloved child, and "you will grow in wisdom and your heart will be drawn into understanding, which will empower you to make right decisions" (v. 19). You always have a second chance.

CHALLENGE: Reread Proverbs 23:17–25. Picture Solomon writing these words to you. Imagine him contemplating how to best encourage and challenge you. Underline the verbs. Which actions catch your attention? Ask God, What life decisions do I need to make? It won't be "three easy lessons on how to live" or "five quick steps to freedom." Your transformation will mean a lifetime of not attempting to follow Him in your own strength but in the strength that the Lord supplies you to do His will (Philippians 2:12–13).

WISDOM'S WARNING

Go and rescue the perishing! Be their savior!
Why would you stand back and watch them stagger to
their death?
And why would you say, "But it's none of my
business"? The one who knows you completely and
judges your every motive is also the keeper of souls—
and not just yours!
He sees through your excuses and holds you responsible
for failing to help those whose lives are threatened.
—PROVERBS 24:11–12

READ: PROVERBS 24:1–22

C ould you have done it? Could you have faced off with Adolf Hitler as he forced six million Jews into slave camps and gas chambers, as the smoke and the stench rose above the ovens?[14] You smirk and say, "That was then, not now. That was there, not here." However, genocide still exists (fortunately no longer here in the United States, though certainly in the past many Native Americans, African-Americans and other minorities have been unjustly persecuted and in many cases even killed.) Will you join the protest or claim ignorance?[15]

What about the sixty million aborted babies who will never see the light of day?[16] Would you join the protests in front of abortion clinics or volunteer at a pregnancy support center? Or do you declare, "I wouldn't do it, but it's a woman's right. It's her body!"?

Would you fight human trafficking—keep an eye out especially for girls and boys (one in five victims are children) who may be caught in the web of sexual exploitation or forced labor? [17] Would you be willing to report the abuser to local authorities or do you turn a blind eye, too fearful to get involved?

Then there are those who are overweight, out-of-fashion, people of color, or just different who get laughed at, bullied, sometimes even beaten. Do you look the other way, unwilling to tangle with the bullies? "It's none of my business." Besides they may jump on you.

Worse yet, what about your neighbors, who have no clue what awaits them if they do not hear the good news?" Are you actually squeamish about sharing yet insisting you're not being led?

But God "sees through your excuses and holds you responsible" (v. 12). That is not a light matter. Jesus said, "'When you refused to help one of the least important among . . . my true brothers and sisters, you refused to help and honor me.' And they will depart from his presence and go into eternal punishment." Matthew 25:45–46).

CHALLENGE: Is there some arena in your life where you know there is injustice? Encourage yourself with this promise, "God will continually revitalize you, implanting within you the passion to do what pleases Him" (Philippians 2:13). Will you join the protest, take action, follow His command? Ask for His desire. Write down what He tells you. Journal your response.

REVELATION FROM THE WISE

God conceals the revelation of his word
in the hiding place of his glory.
But the honor of kings is revealed
by how they thoroughly search out
the deeper meaning of all that God says.
—PROVERBS 25:2

READ: PROVERBS 24:23–PROVERBS 25:14

You and some of your close friends are lying on the beach looking skyward. It's a clear dark night with a thumbnail moon and stars sprinkled across the sky like sand. Someone points out the Big Dipper and Venus. "You think you could touch them, but they are light-years away!" You shake your head in wonder. "One light year is six trillion miles. That is a six with twelve zeroes after it! And that is 2,400,000 treks around the earth!"

Have you ever looked at the heavens through a telescope? What about the Hubble Space Telescope?[18] Ours is not the only galaxy. Now we can see millions of them. We observe the birth of new stars, discover planets outside our solar system, view super massive black holes, a nebula stretching across the sky 110 light-years in length, super nova explosions, and pulsars. It blows your mind!

"Well, it is God's creation. It's bound to be as breathtaking as He is. But do you ever wonder how He did it? I mean, do you think He only spoke it into being? 'Let there be light' and—bingo!—there was light. That sounds like the Big Bang theory. Do you think He'll reveal His secret, how He really did it?" (see Genesis 1:3).

"I don't think so. Isaiah tells us God likes to hide Himself. It keeps us in awe of Him" (Isaiah 45:15) But maybe in eternity He'll explain.

CHALLENGE: Take some friends and go to a spot far away from city lights; play some worship music (anybody play guitar?), and gaze into the night sky. What is God revealing to you about Himself?

WISDOM PRACTICES SELF-CONTROL

If you live without restraint . . . ,
you're as helpless as a city with broken-down defenses,
open to attack.
—PROVERBS 25:28

READ: PROVERBS 25:15–28

Self-control is a fruit of the Holy Spirit, but that means as a follower of Jesus Christ you must walk in the Spirit in order to have self-control (Galatians 5:22–24). The choice is yours. With those who purposefully provoke you, when you need to bite your tongue and treat them with kindness in their time of need, God will reward you. For example, the king of Aram was at war with Israel, and Elisha, the prophet, continually thwarted his plans. When the king sought to destroy Elisha, he and his whole army were blinded and captured. The king of Israel wanted to kill them. But Elisha insisted that the trapped Aramean army be given a great feast and then sent home. The fruit? "The bands from Aram stopped raiding Israel's territory" (2 Kings 6:23 NIV).

Reread Proverbs 25:15–28, and you'll discover other arenas to practice self-control. Are you prone to overindulge in sweets or overstay your welcome? Do you seek the praise of those around you or slander your colleagues? Worse still, do you compromise your moral standards, thus contaminating your life as well as the lives of those who know you?

Be encouraged: "As you yield freely and fully to the dynamic life and power of the Holy Spirit, you will abandon the cravings of your self-life" (Galatians 5:16). As you walk with God, you will have self-control.

CHALLENGE: Do you lack self-control in any areas of your life? Think it through; make a list. Then repair the breach; ask the Lord for specific directions. The fruit: you will not be "helpless as a city with broken-down defenses, open to attack" (v. 28).

DON'T BE A FOOL

There's only one thing worse than a fool,
and that's the smug, conceited man
always in love with his own opinions.
—PROVERBS 26:12

READ: PROVERBS 26:1–12

Everything you ever wanted to know about fools is found here in these verses. But alas, believe it or not, one can be worse than a fool!

She enters the classroom, chin up, smiling condescendingly at her fellow students. She considers herself the top of the class, but a "conceited ignoramus" is what they whisper behind her back.

He calls the meeting to order with the sound of his gavel. A member proffers a suggestion. The CEO chuckles, "In my opinion that will not fly. Here's what we should do." The board members exchange glances. "Here we go again. I wonder how far he'd get without us picking up the pieces?"

The danger of this disease of pride and conceit is it blinds us to our greatest need, our need for God. Like the proud Pharisees, we flaunt our faith as a religious cloak covering up the reality of our blindness. If only we allowed ourselves to see our imperfections, then we could humbly receive from God the grace we need to navigate life.

CHALLENGE: Is it possible that you are prone to being "worse than a fool" (v. 12), convinced you are always right? If yes, acknowledge your pride today and humble yourself before the Lord. (This was Lucifer's problem, the "anointed cherub." Check it out in Ezekiel 28:13–17.)

DON'T BE LAZY

The lazy loafer says, "I can't go out and look for a job
. . the lazy man keeps turning over, hinged to his bed!
There are some people so lazy they won't even work to
feed themselves.
—PROVERBS 26:13–15

READ: PROVERBS 26:13–17

You've met them, and hopefully you're not among them, the young men and women afraid to begin the job search. Even those with degrees will sometimes hide behind the academic walls, unwilling to test the waters.

Then there are those who just can't get up in the morning after spending most of the night gaming or scanning social media. No amount of coffee can unhinge them from their beds.

What about the able bodied—that's who Solomon says "won't even work to feed themselves" (v. 15)—who visit the food pantries or the churches that serve hot lunches to the homeless?

Why not do an online job search. Or maybe you need to learn to cook!

"But," you ask, "what about resting? Is that consider being lazy? Didn't God work for six days and then rest on the seventh? Isn't that one of the Ten Commandments?" As long as we are working the other six, God says take a day. He wants us to live a balanced life, and it stands to reason we should mirror the actions of our Father.

CHALLENGE: Do you find yourself putting off till tomorrow what could or should be done today? Is the reason fear, wrong choices, or indeed laziness? What about your "day of rest"—does it honor the Lord? Examine yourself under the Holy Spirit's guidance. He will lead you to the truth. Then take action.

WATCH YOUR WORDS

Your words are so powerful that they will kill or give life.
—PROVERBS 18:21

READ: PROVERBS 26:18–28

Do you ever wonder why Solomon put so much focus on the tongue? And in these verses, he lists almost every scenario possible of misusing our words. It undoubtedly describes how his seven hundred wives and three hundred concubines got along with each other (see 1 Kings 11:3). Even just two wives can cause bitter conflict and hurt; just consider Rachel and Leah (Genesis 29:11–Genesis 30:24) or Elkanah's two wives, one being Samuel's mother (1 Samuel 1:1–7).

However, hurtful words don't just occur between wives of the Old Testament. Colleagues at work, roommates at school, fellow soldiers in the army— all of us can rip one another apart with our words. It just takes a dagger at the tip of the tongue.

Apparently, in Solomon's eyes the one he most wants to expose is the hypocrite—the one whose corrupt heart is covered with a cheap glaze. He's not kidding when he writes that "one day [the hypocrite's] hypocrisy will be exposed before all the world" (v. 26)! Jesus Himself proclaimed, "You can be sure of this: when the day of judgment comes, everyone will be held accountable for every careless word he has spoken. Your very words will be used as evidence against you, and your words will declare you either innocent or guilty" (Matthew 12:36–37).

CHALLENGE: Now read verses 18–22 and 27–28 for other ways the tongue can be misused. Are you guilty? Have you ever "accidentally" gossiped while sharing a prayer request? Surely your goal is to let all that you say and do "be drenched with the beauty of our Lord Jesus" (Colossians 3:17). Confess where you have failed in any way—in fact, write it out—and ask to be forgiven (1 John 1:9).

HEED WISDOM'S WARNINGS

Just as no two faces are exactly alike,
so every heart is different.
—PROVERBS 27:19

READ: PROVERBS 27

As you read through this chapter, you'll discover a variety of life lessons. Jot down the references for any that are meaningful to you. This is the Holy Spirit attempting to speak to your heart.

For example, consider verse 1. Maybe you need to learn the lesson of making plans, considering them guaranteed, when in reality you haven't a clue what tomorrow holds. Instead you should say, if the Lord wills, we will still be alive and able to carry out this plan (James 4:13–15).

Or how about verse 4—are your coworkers jealous of you, or are you jealous of them?

Verses 5–6 touch on being teachable. How do you handle it when your best friend corrects you? Are you resentful or grateful?

Such friendships should be treasured, as iron sharpens iron—just as "one person sharpens another" (Proverbs 27:17 NIV).

Verse 18 relates to workplace performance. What rating did you get on your last employee evaluation? If you served your boss, your manager, the CEO well, chances are, you'll get a raise or perhaps a promotion. Diligence pays off.

Verse 14 is the funniest of the lot: "Do you think you're blessing your neighbors when you sing at the top of your lungs early in the morning?" If you're in the shower, your roommate may understand. But otherwise, "singing" at the wrong time, in the wrong manner, can be interpreted as insincere or as a jab intended to hurt.

This is only a sampling of the wisdom Solomon has to offer in Proverbs 27. Choosing to walk in that wisdom is proof that you have not been taught in vain (v. 11).

CHALLENGE: Hopefully at least one of the twenty-seven verses in Proverbs 27 spoke to you. Take that one, record it, making note of what the Holy Spirit speaks to your heart. Then do as He has instructed.

DEVO 59

LOVERS OF GOD

Overjoyed is the one who
with tender heart trembles before God.
—PROVERBS 28:14

READ: PROVERBS 28

What does it mean to be a lover of God?

It means we will not fear people. Even if all our friends tease us for our Christian values, for our unwillingness to bend the rules, we fear God.

It means we will serve God and not self, for that is the purpose of life. We may not do so perfectly, but His will, His purpose, is our desire. We want to please Him.

It means we will choose to be upright in our dealings with others. No one can accuse us of having cheated them or given them false information. Our God does not lie, and we desire to walk in His way.

It means if we have a position of leadership, we will lead with the intent to benefit those under our authority. Our constituents will not need to hide. We represent the King of the universe Who is Himself love.

It means we love the Lord with all our heart, all our soul, all our mind, and all our strength (Mark 12:30). No half measures. He died for us while we were yet sinners; we can't help but love Him (Romans 5:8).

CHALLENGE: As one who has chosen to be a lover of God, go back and read those verses in Proverbs 28 that relate to loving God (verses 1, 5, 10, 12, 14) in order to discover the benefits of being a lover of God. Write in your own words what these benefits are.

DON'T BE STUBBORN

Stubborn people who repeatedly
refuse to accept correction
will suddenly be broken and never recover.
—PROVERBS 29:1

READ: PROVERBS 29:1–7

"Suddenly" . . . "never recover" (v. 1). These words freeze us in our tracks; fear threatens to engulf us. "Stubborn" can be a good trait (v. 1). It can mean we will persist, never give up, accomplish our goal. Unfortunately, the goal here is to "refuse to accept correction" (v. 1). It's our nature, our sin nature, that we are born with. We want to do our own thing.

Hopefully, our parents haven't "spared the rod" and we've been corrected (see Proverbs 13:24). But if they didn't succeed, maybe being sent to the principal's office or sitting in detention or getting out-of-school suspensions and thus missing ball practice (maybe even getting kicked off the team) caused us to wise up.

Next comes the job market. Bosses don't put up with defiance too long before we find ourselves demoted or fired, without a positive reference for future work. The future looks bleak, hopefully bleak enough for us to learn to accept correction.

But the one who continues stubbornly to ignore the redirection, the invitations of the Father, our ultimate parent, will "suddenly be broken and never recover" (v. 1). The evening news will announce our death; there's no more recourse.

There's no more recourse—unless we respond to the nudging of the Holy Spirit and have a change of heart.

CHALLENGE: Do you have a loved one, friend, or acquaintance who stubbornly refuses to respond to the gospel? Intercede for them. Ask the Holy Spirit to convict them that the world is wrong (John 16:8). Both heaven and hell are real. Plead with the Father. Remind Him that He desires no one should perish (Matthew 18:14). Let us also be salt and light. Our lives should make others cry out, "I want what you've got!" (Matthew 5:13–17).

YOU CAN'T ARGUE WITH A FOOL

Arrogant cynics love to pick fights, but the humble
and wise love to pursue peace.
There's no use arguing with a fool,
for his ranting and raving prevent you
from making a case and
settling the argument in a calm way.
Violent men hate those with integrity, but
the lovers of God esteem those who are holy.
—PROVERBS 29:8–10

READ: PROVERBS 29:8–27

The closed garage, the practice room for a little-known band in Louisiana, stank from body odor as harsh words spewed out of the bass guitarist's mouth. "How can you guys be so behind the times! Rock and roll went out the window decades ago."

"Listen, I was just in Nashville last year and rock and roll is still in."

"But we are not in Nashville; we are fifty miles north of New Orleans. Pop is the way to go. You guys are just stick-in-the muds. I'm tempted to take my bass elsewhere."

"Come on. We have a gig coming up."

"Then play my kind of music or . . ."

Meanwhile, on the other side of the continent, an on-stage sound engineer for a nationally known band had recently come to faith. The drummer began to complain, "He screwed me over last night."

"Are you sure? That doesn't sound like him."

"Well, since he's become a Jesus freak, he's not the same."

"What? If anything, he's better."

"That's your opinion. I want him out of here!"

"But he's really valuable."

"Well, I'm not bending. You know the rules. We all have to be on the same page."

And the rule meant that the sound engineer had to be let go.

CHALLENGE: The Lord loves the cynic and the men who hate those with integrity as much as He loves you. Do you know anyone like this who always demands his way or no way? Even if you don't, how would you reach out to such a one? For starters, check out Matthew 5, especially verses 38–48. With the leading of the Holy Spirit, make a plan for how to reach out to those caught in insisting on their own will. Record the results.

THE MYSTERIOUS SAYINGS OF AGUR

God, I'm so weary and worn-out,
I feel more like a beast than a man. . . .
I've yet to learn the wisdom
that comes from the full and intimate knowledge of
you, the Holy One.
—PROVERBS 30:2–3

READ: PROVERBS 30:1–3

C an you identify with Agur? You want an intimate relationship with God, and yet it seems beyond your grasp. You want to live like Christ, and you read that "there remains no accusing voice of condemnation against those who are joined in life-union with Jesus" (Romans 8:1). But the voice of condemnation still seems loud and clear: you blew it last night and again this morning and feel beastly (v. 2). You are weary from trying.

Yet you nevertheless find yourself drawn to the Holy One. His omniscience, His omnipresence, His omnipotence, this great infinite Creator God—oh, how wonderful it would be to have "full and intimate knowledge" of Him (v. 3)!

So how do you learn to be intimately acquainted with the God of the universe? First, it's important to recognize that intimacy with God is not an academic exercise. He is Father, Son, and Holy Spirit. He put that longing in your heart to enjoy His presence since before the foundation of the world for He desires that relationship as much as you! Such intimacy is achieved only by personal revelation from the Holy Spirit, who is the ultimate teacher (John 14:26).

CHALLENGE: Where are you in your relationship with God? Are you hot, cold, indifferent? Ask the Holy Spirit to tell you. Write down what He says and then go from there.

SIX QUESTIONS

Who is it that travels back and forth
from the heavenly realm to the earth?
Who controls the wind as it blows
and holds it in his fists?
Who tucks the rain into the cloak of his clouds?
Who stretches out the skyline from one vista to the
other? What is his name? And what is the name of his
Son? Who can tell me?
—PROVERBS 30:4

READ: PROVERBS 30:4

W*ho is it that travels back and forth from the heavenly realm to the earth?*
Elohim, who is not bound by space or time, who visits His people when He pleases (see Genesis 1:1–2, where the name is first used; Genesis 11:5 is an example).

Who controls the wind as it blows and holds it in his fists?

El Shaddai, the God Almighty, who holds our future and can make the wind blow wherever He wishes (see Genesis 28:3; e.g. Genesis 8:1).

Who tucks the rain into the cloak of his clouds?

Adonai, the compassionate Lord, who showers us with blessing but does not let the guilty go unpunished (see Numbers 14:17–18; e.g. Genesis 7:1).

Who stretches out the skyline from one vista to the other?

El Roi, the God who sees and watches over all His creation (see Genesis 16:13–14; e.g. Genesis 16:7–11).

What is his name?

Yahweh, the unspeakable Name, with unlimited majesty, who chose me to be His own and to protect me always (see Isaiah 43:1; e.g. Psalm 91:1–13).

And what is the name of his Son?

Jesus, the Savior, the Christ, the one who came from above and is above all things. (John 3:31)

Who can tell me?

I can! For I have been raised up with Christ the exalted One and am now seated with Him in the heavenly realm (Ephesians 2:6).

CHALLENGE: These are only a few of the names of God. Which, if any, are meaningful to you and why?

GOING DEEPER: You can read about more of these names in the Names of God (NOG) Bible. Check out Exodus 34:5–7 to discover how the Lord lists His own attributes.

A PURE HEART IS FILLED WITH GOD'S WORD

Every promise from the faithful God
is pure and proves to be true.
He is a wrap-around shield of protection
for all his lovers who run to hide in him.
Never add to his words, or he will have to rebuke you
and prove that you're a liar.
—PROVERBS 30:5–6

READ: PROVERBS 30:5–17

You often feel weary at the end of a day bombarded by trials (your roommate's dog couldn't hold it in; your coworker was incessantly complaining; you received anxious texts from your mom almost every hour). Where do you seek comfort, relief, a shield of protection—your favorite ice cream or maybe a workout at the gym?

Unfortunately, we have an enemy who "roams around incessantly, like a roaring lion looking for its prey to devour" (1 Peter 5:8). Neither ice cream nor the gym stands a chance against him. We need to pick up the sword of the Spirit, which is the Word of God! Weakened at the end of a forty-day fast, that's what Jesus used to knock out the enemy (see Matthew 4:1–11). That is where our protection lies.

Our protection lies in God's Word unless we attempt to add to it (v. 6). When we drift from the truth, a generation arises and bears fruit for the enemy. For example, slave owners and later segregationists claimed that Ephesians 6:5 (NASB)—"Slaves, be obedient to . . . your masters"—gave them the right to consider blacks no better than animals and oftentimes treated them worse! Even now, ignoring His Word gives the homosexual community authority in the church (see Romans 1:24–27). How does the Author respond? He will rebuke us to encourage us to repent and avoid the fate of liars, which is "the lake of fire" (Revelation 21:8).

As we face our daily trials using the Word of God, let us also put on the helmet of salvation to redirect our thoughts from the onset.

CHALLENGE: Where in the Word can we find comfort and strength and hope in times of trial? Try the Psalms; David was often confronted with trials, but he made the Lord his shelter (Psalm 91). Words from the Lord initially given to Israel can strengthen you as well (see Isaiah 43:1–21). In the New Testament, we are instructed to cast our cares upon the Lord (1 Peter 5:7) and make our requests known to God with thanksgiving (Philippians 4:6–7). Test out these verses, and then add them to your arsenal.

FOUR MYSTERIES

There are four marvelous mysteries . . .
The way an eagle flies in the sky,
the way a snake glides on a boulder,
the path of a ship as it passes through the sea, and
the way a bridegroom falls in love with his bride.
—PROVERBS 30:18–19

READ: PROVERBS 30:18–20

Here are four snapshots that can represent these "four marvelous mysteries" (v. 18):

There's the picture of the eagle soaring above the earth. Resting on the currents of the air, his gaze is focused on the Lord awaiting His instruction. Thus, he does not grow weary as he swoops down again and again to snare his sustenance (see Isaiah 40:28–31).

Next, we see a snake slithering upon a rock—the same snake that ensnared Eve in the garden. This alludes to our sin, which is abolished when we place our faith in the Rock, Christ Jesus.

The third image is of a ship, full sail on the high seas. Its destination lies ahead. We witness God's power in breathtaking sunsets; then we are tossed about like spinning tops. We cry out with fear. He stills the storm and guides us to a safe haven by His lights in the heavens (Psalm 107:23–30).

Finally, we have the image that thrills our hearts—the mystery of true love! Who can explain what attracts a man to a particular woman? What is even more mind-boggling is the love of our heavenly Bridegroom who chooses us and draws us to Himself (Ephesians 5:32).

CHALLENGE: Do any of these snapshots reflect your current life circumstances? If yes, how so? If not, then read the scriptures accompanying each snapshot and select the one that most speaks to you and share why.

FOUR INTOLERABLE THINGS

There are four intolerable events
that are simply unbearable to observe.
—PROVERBS 30:21

READ: PROVERBS 30:21–23

Described in these verses are four "friends" you don't want to have, also four people you don't want to become.

There's the fellow employee who backstabs his cohorts and wheedles his way into being the manager. He becomes arrogant and imperious, drunk with the power of his new position.

There's the so-called friend who's always borrowing and rarely repaying yet secretly has come into a significant inheritance. Or maybe he flaunts his recently attained wealth, belittling those around him.

Next, perhaps you know a woman who loves to flirt and some really nice guy marries her! She insists that the other men she's connected with are "just friends" and "what's wrong with flirting?"

But the one that truly breaks your heart is the woman who seduces her best friend's husband and ends up married to him. Was he, too, at fault? No matter, she lit the fire.

CHALLENGE: Hopefully none of these describe you, but if they do, repent and ask forgiveness from those affected by your behavior. However, instead you may have a friend, one who claims to be a follower of Christ, in one of these categories. You have a responsibility to go to that one (see Galatians 6:1), but before you do, read Ephesians 4:29. If the friend does not repent, then follow the advice in Matthew 18:16–17. In either event, record your actions.

FOUR CREATURES SMALL AND WISE

The earth has four creatures that are very small
but very wise:
The feeble ant . . . The delicate rock-badger . . .
The locusts . . . And the small lizard.
—PROVERBS 30:24–28

READ: PROVERBS 30:24–28

Are you like an ant—industrious, knowing how to prepare for the future? Or more like a rock-badger who climbs to the top of peaks on lookout for the enemy's approach, warning your friends of imminent danger? Maybe you are part of the brotherhood of locusts working in unity to achieve any purpose, defeat any foe. God can always use a person with any of these attributes. But what about the lizard?

Lizards, in general, don't like being easy to catch. They get stressed out about being handled at all. Where does such a one— who is fearful, anxious, prone to slip away—fit into the kingdom scheme of things? Yet he does indeed have a place in the king's palace! In fact, "God chose the puny and powerless to shame the high and mighty" (1 Corinthians 1:27).

Being "small" does not define who we are. We all have purpose whether we represent the ant, the rock-badger, the locust, or the lizard. In fact, no follower of Jesus is without purpose in this life. God has already prepared good works for you to do. "Even before we were born, God planned . . . our destiny and [what] we would do to fulfill it" (Ephesians 2:10).

CHALLENGE: Do you see yourself as insignificant (like the small lizard) and therefore do not pursue the "good works" God has planned for you to do (Ephesians 2:10)? Perhaps there is some "good work" you feel drawn to but feel you can't do it? Consider drawing your strength and wisdom from the Lord (see Philippians 4:13 and James 1:5) Take inventory: is there something you should be doing? If so, why are you not doing it?

FOUR STATELY THINGS

There are four stately monarchs . . .
the lion, the king of the jungle, who is afraid of no
one, the rooster strutting boldly among the hens,
the male goat out in front leading the herd,
and a king leading his regal procession.
—PROVERBS 30:29–31

READ: PROVERBS 30:29–33

You're definitely not a lion or a rooster or a goat, and probably not a king, but you could be a manager of a profitable business, a quarterback for a winning team, or head nurse in a top-rated Intensive Care Unit.

And if the images are meant to be a description of different types of leaders in the world, what do they stir in your soul? How do you feel? Unruffled? Self-confident? Fearless? Prosperous? Dignified? Triumphant? Regal? Majestic with a train following your lead? Possibly you feel proud, for who can surpass you?

But hold it. Stop right there. Pride can lead to self-exaltation. Self-exaltation can lead to the abuse of power. Abuse of power can lead to strife, an uprising against one of the "stately monarchs" (v. 29). This is not the kingdom way. Nor is it the direction you want your business or your team or your organization to take.

Be a servant leader. Be like Jesus who was a great teacher yet washed the feet of His students, His team. He observed that in the daily wear and tear of life, one can become tired or short-tempered or despairing. His ministry was to refresh, to cleanse, to cheer on those who served under Him. As Jesus said, "now put into practice what I have done" (John 13:17).

CHALLENGE: What is your current status in life? If you are in any position of leadership (president of a corporation or manager of an assembly line or head nurse in an ICU), how are you handling it? Are you a servant leader? If not, make a new plan. Trust in the Lord to direct you toward acts of service that will bless those who work under you.

INSPIRED WORDS

These are the inspired words my mother taught me.
—PROVERBS 31:1

READ: PROVERBS 31:1–9

This mom is passionate about her son. But isn't that generally the case with moms and sons, even dads and daughters? Her advice we've heard before: stay sexually pure, don't get drunk, and treat the poor and defenseless with honor. It's even repeated in the New Testament. We are "to make a difference in the lives of the orphans, and widows in their troubles, and refuse to be corrupted by the world's values" (James 1:27).

Three times, this mom refers to her son as a king. She's ambitious for him—a true picture of many moms. She knows that illicit relationships can cost a man his role of leadership. (Reread Solomon's advice to his son in Devo 17.) She knows that drunkenness befuddles the mind, weakens the will. (Reread Solomon's warning in Devo 51.) She knows, too, if he lacks compassion and overlooks the needs of the poor, he'll be in big trouble! (Proverbs 17:5).

You are probably not being groomed to be a king or a queen, but this advice is just as pertinent for you. We all lead, whether as a role model for younger siblings, as captain of our soccer team, as manager of a retail store, or as CEO of an upscale corporation. Even if you didn't have a mom that taught you these things, follow what this mom in Proverbs 31 has taught her son; her inspired words will also benefit you.

CHALLENGE: In what arenas or ways are you playing a leadership role? With the Holy Spirit's guidance, examine yourself. Do you value staying sexually pure, walking in sobriety, and treating the poor and defenseless with honor? If convicted, turn from any sins and ask the Lord to help you grow into a godly leader. Note: Ladies these words apply for you as well!

THE RADIANT BRIDE

Let us rejoice and exalt [the Lord our God]
and give him glory, because
the wedding celebration of the Lamb has come.
And his bride has made herself ready.
—REVELATION 19:7

This virtuous woman lives in the wonder,
awe, and fear of the Lord.
She will be praised throughout eternity . . .
for she has become a radiant woman.
—PROVERBS 31:30–31

READ: PROVERBS 31:10–31; REVELATION 19:6–8

Are you aware that this radiant bride is you? Male and female together, the body of Christ, the Church, is the bride of Christ? And your Bridegroom eagerly awaits you in heaven.

But prior to the wedding celebration, there "will be a time of great misery beyond the magnitude of anything the world has ever seen" (Matthew 24:21). This bride must be a valiant warrior (v. 29)! Dressed in the armor of God, she will not be dissuaded from doing good deeds, from feeding the hungry—both spiritually and physically—from helping the poor, even her enemies (v. 15, 17, 20, 24). No matter how dark the night, her light will not be extinguished (v. 18). She laughs at the future (v. 25)!

Her Bridegroom paid a great price for her—His very own blood. But He has no regrets. She does not disgrace His name but rather enhances His fame, always seeking to do what is pure in the eyes of her Bridegroom.

Does your heart pound within you as you consider that this is you? This is who you are, because your heavenly Bridegroom lives within you. He is your "heavenly treasure chest of hope" (Colossians 1:27). You will be praised throughout eternity, the radiant bride reigning at the side of the King of Glory.

CHALLENGE: The book of Proverbs ends as it began (compare Proverbs 1:7 and Proverbs 31:30) that the most significant goal you can come away with, the most trustworthy advice, the heartbeat of God's GPS is to fear and obey the Lord. In your opinion, what does it mean to fear the Lord? Consider Matthew 22:37 and John 14:15. Are you en route to becoming a "radiant bride"? Set specific goals to make it a reality.

THE JOURNEY IS OVER

Well, we made it! Despite a few detours here and there, some course correction, our destination is here. Yet the road continues on. We'll make use of "God's GPS," but this time it'll be His Word and His Holy Spirit to guide us on our journey.

It may also be useful to review some of the wisdom we gleaned from God's GPS. When a circumstance crops up and we recall, "Ah, yes, I remember that was addressed. Let me thumb through the devotional and find it."

I, the author, would like to get to know you, but not just your name and address. Where are you in life? Is your way easy or tough? What are your hopes for the future? Are you still a single young adult?

I'd also like to hear your response to God's GPS. Did it have any impact on your thinking, your choices? Which was your favorite devotion? Which was your least favorite and why? By all means, tell me the truth.

You can contact me at godsgps22@gmail.com. I look forward to hearing from you.

DEVO 1

❧

_____

_____

_____

_____

_____

_____

_____

_____

_____

_____

_____

_____

_____

_____

_____

DEVO 2

࿇

DEVO 3

DEVO 4

DEVO 5

❧

_____

_____

_____

_____

_____

_____

_____

_____

_____

_____

_____

_____

_____

_____

_____

DEVO 6

❦

_____

_____

_____

_____

_____

_____

_____

_____

_____

_____

_____

_____

_____

_____

DEVO 7

DEVO 8

DEVO 9

~~

___

___

___

___

___

___

___

___

___

___

___

___

___

DEVO 10

❧

_____

_____

_____

_____

_____

_____

_____

_____

_____

_____

_____

_____

DEVO 11

DEVO 12

❧

DEVO 13

DEVO 14

❧

_____

_____

_____

_____

_____

_____

_____

_____

_____

_____

_____

_____

DEVO 15

DEVO 16

DEVO 17

～

_____

_____

_____

_____

_____

_____

_____

_____

_____

_____

_____

_____

_____

DEVO 18

DEVO 19

༄

_____

_____

_____

_____

_____

_____

_____

_____

_____

_____

_____

_____

_____

_____

DEVO 20

෨

DEVO 21

&

❧

DEVO 23

❧

❦

DEVO 25

❧

_____

_____

_____

_____

_____

_____

_____

_____

_____

_____

_____

_____

DEVO 27

❧

_____

_____

_____

_____

_____

_____

_____

_____

_____

_____

_____

_____

_____

DEVO 28

DEVO 29

❧

❦

_____

_____

_____

_____

_____

_____

_____

_____

_____

_____

_____

DEVO 31

~∂

_____

_____

_____

_____

_____

_____

_____

_____

_____

_____

_____

_____

_____

❧

DEVO 33

❧

DEVO 35

DEVO 36

DEVO 37

DEVO 38

DEVO 39

࿐

_____

_____

_____

_____

_____

_____

_____

_____

_____

_____

_____

_____

DEVO 40

⧽

DEVO 41

DEVO 42

৵

DEVO 43

DEVO 44

DEVO 45

༄

_____

_____

_____

_____

_____

_____

_____

_____

_____

_____

_____

_____

_____

_____

DEVO 46

&

DEVO 47

❧

_____

_____

_____

_____

_____

_____

_____

_____

_____

_____

_____

_____

_____

_____

_____

DEVO 48

❧

DEVO 49

❦

DEVO 50

᠀

_____

_____

_____

_____

_____

_____

_____

_____

_____

_____

_____

_____

DEVO 51

ॐ

DEVO 52

∽

_____

_____

_____

_____

_____

_____

_____

_____

_____

_____

_____

_____

DEVO 53

સ

DEVO 55

ॐ

DEVO 57

DEVO 58

❧

DEVO 59

~

DEVO 60

❧

DEVO 61

෴

_____

_____

_____

_____

_____

_____

_____

_____

_____

_____

_____

_____

_____

DEVO 62

DEVO 63

DEVO 64

❧

DEVO 65

DEVO 67

❧

_____

_____

_____

_____

_____

_____

_____

_____

_____

_____

_____

_____

_____

_____

༺

DEVO 69

DEVO 70

ABOUT THE AUTHOR

Vera Brennan is a retired math teacher by default, who decided to make the most of her retirement by writing. (Her first love was writing, but she was told by her high school guidance counselor that English teachers come a dime a dozen however as a math teacher, she would always have a job. It proved true.) She holds a bachelor's degree in math education and a master's in broadcasting disciplines earned at University of North Carolina, Chapel Hill.

Having a love for Israel—as well as adventure—Vera spent a year on a kibbutz outside Haifa during the Yom Kippur War in 1973. She returned, four years later, for a seven-month stint in Jerusalem to research for her master's thesis, a documentary on the Messianic congregation established there at the end of the nineteenth century.

She also lived for two shorter periods in the Galilee area. During this time, Vera joined a Messianic community in northern Minnesota for four years and from there moved to Brooklyn where she worked in Manhattan.

Then came Vera's final destination: Kingston, New York. She returned to teaching at a local community college, where she became involved with BASIC college ministries (Brothers and Sisters in Christ) by bringing it to her campus. In 1990 Vera married, but the adventures did not cease. The two became involved with indigenous churches in the Philippines and Mexico, making numerous trips to both countries. In Mexico, they participate in events led by and for single young adults. To celebrate their twenty-fifth wedding anniversary, they joined a group of single young adults serving at a children's camp in Bosnia-Herzegovina—undoubtedly one of their most eye-opening adventures.

At home Vera facilitates women's Bible studies, does evangelistic outreaches with other local churches as well as premarital and marital counseling alongside her husband. They have two grown sons and four grandchildren. The older son's testimony of his encounter with Proverbs as a single young adult is the inspiration for this devotional.

Her retirement has been far from dull, replete with acts of service and writing as she personally uses God's GPS!

ENDNOTES

1   For more details and to read support for The Passion Translation, go to https://www.thepassiontranslation. com/endorsements/.

2   Dr. Elana Yael Heideman, "Israel and the Meaning of 70," The Israel Foundation, accessed October 26, 2022, https://israelforever.org/interact/blog/israel_ and_the_meaning_of_70.

3   Lily Rothman, "Is God Dead? At 50," Time.com, accessed October, 26, 2022,

4   Julia Haines, Kaia Hubbard, and Christopher Wolf, "Where State Abortion Laws Stand without Roe," USNews.com, December 2, 2022, https://www. usnews.com/news/best-states/articles/a-guide-to- abortion-laws-by-state.

5   "The Journey to Marriage Equality in the United States," Human Rights Campaign, accessed December 7, 2022, https://www.hrc.org/our-work/ stories/the-journey-to-marriage-equality-in-the- united-states.

6   Michael R. Sisak, "22 Mass Shootings. 374 Dead. Here's Where the Guns Came From," APNews. com, May 27, 2022, https://apnews.com/article/ uvalde-school-shooting-buffalo-supermarket-texas- d1415e5a50eb85a50d5464970a225b2d.

7   "Discernment for Dummies Part 1: What Is
         Discernment," MGL Priests and Brothers, YouTube
         video, November 30, 2014, https://www.youtube.
         com/watch?v=8yaprUS1RrY, and "Discernment
         for Dummies Part 2: Falling in Love with Jesus,"
         MGL Priests and Brothers, YouTube video,
         November 30, 2014, https://www.youtube.com/
         watch?v=PXPWkzQX23I.

8   For evidence and more details, go to https://www.
         psychologytoday.com/us/blog/fulfillment-any-
         age/201303/how-casual-sex-can-affect-our-mental-
         health and https://fightthenewdrug.org/3-reasons-
         why-watching-porn-is-harmful/.

9   Scott Stanley, "Sliding vs. Deciding: Cohabitation,
         Relationship Development, and Commitment,"
         Wheatley Institute, YouTube video, April 17, 2015,
         https://youtu.be/5TpuIWdy6aE.

10   Elias Scully, "21 Day Habit Timeline: How to Form
         a Habit in 21 Days (Day by Day!)," Medium.com,
         August 6, 2019, https://medium.com/swlh/21-day-
         habit-timeline-how-to-form-a-habit-in-days-day-by-
         day-92298446bf6b.

11   Dave Kraft, "True Leaders Are Teachable,"
         TheGospelCoalition.org, July 2, 2016, https://
         www.thegospelcoalition.org/article/true-leaders-are-
         teachable/.

12   David Henderson, "Lord Acton on 'Power
         Corrupts,'" Econlib.com, blog post, February 18,
         2013, https://www.econlib.org/archives/2013/02/
         lord_acton_on_p.html.

13   Derek Prince, "God's Medicine Bottle," YouTube
      video, December 3, 2018, https://www.youtube.
      com/watch?v=b4meQl9Mn4k.

14   "Documenting Numbers of Victims of the Holocaust
      and Nazi Persecution," Holocaust Encyclopedia,
      last edited December 8, 2020, https://encyclopedia.
      ushmm.org/content/en/article/documenting-
      numbers-of-victims-of-the-holocaust-and-nazi-
      persecution.

15   Find out more details at GenocideWatch.com about
      genocides occurring around the world.

16   "U.S. Abortion Statistics: Facts and Figured Relating
      to the Frequency of Abortion in the United States,"
      Abort73.com, updated June 23, 2022, accessed
      November 5, 2022, https://abort73.com/abortion_
      facts/us_abortion_statistics/.

17   "What Is Human Trafficking?," ICE.gov, U.S.
      Immigration and Customs Enforcement, Official
      Website of the Department of Homeland Security,
      accessed November 5, 2022, https://www.ice.gov/
      features/human-trafficking.

18   Go to https://hubblesite.org/resource-gallery/images
      for some amazing photos from NASA.

CPSIA information can be obtained
at www.ICGtesting.com
Printed in the USA
BVHW030257010323
659387BV00009B/495

9 781959 099116